SHOTSHELLS
AND
CEDAR SHAFTS

SHOTSHELLS
AND
CEDAR SHAFTS

Outdoor Adventures
with Shotgun
and Recurve Bow

Bruce A. Hopkins

Illustrated by Tom Yacovella

Cassety Hollow Publishing

ISBN: 0-9722709-0-6

Published by
Cassety Hollow Publishing
P.O. Box 415
Oriskany Falls, NY 13425-0415

Book and Cover Design: 1106 Design, LLC
Edited by Kate von Seeburg

Cover Photos: White-tailed Deer, Wood Duck, Ring-necked Pheasant and Autumn Forest by Eric Dresser.
Elk by David Olsen

Illustrated by Tom Yacovella

First Edition

A number of the chapters in this book have appeared in print previously. The original versions of "The Bulls of Wolf Lake" and "Just a Short Walk in the Woods" were published in *Traditional Bowhunter*. "Tar Sand, Muskeg and Bears" and "From My Perch in the Woods" appeared in *The Professional Bowhunter Magazine*. "A Buck for Justin" was published in *Full Draw*.

The following trademarks appear throughout this book: G&H, Glo-Mitts, Great Northern, Ithaca, Loc-On, McKenzie, Montgomery Ward, Remington, Robertson Stykbow, Skyline, Super Ghost, Trius, WesternField, Winchester and Zwickey.

Printed in the United States of America

Library of Congress Control Number: 2002092888

TABLE OF CONTENTS

DEDICATION

*This book is dedicated to
Beth, Melissa, Justin and Mom.
Your love and support
make me a very lucky man.*

ACKNOWLEDGEMENTS

No one accomplishes an undertaking of any consequence without the support and assistance of others. I am no different in this respect and wish to pass along my heartfelt thanks to those who have helped me make this book a reality.

I am forever indebted to my wife, Beth, and daughter, Melissa, for completing the word-processing of the initial manuscript. I would also like to thank them, along with my son, Justin, and mother, Marjorie, for reading, and listening to me read, innumerable drafts of each chapter. My thanks and appreciation also goes to my friend, Don Pettit, for reviewing my stories and providing editorial commentary.

A thank you also goes to my sister, Peg, who, probably unbeknownst to her, planted the seeds of encouragement for me to write this book.

I also need to remember the many hunting partners I have shared field, forest and marsh with over the years. Each of them has taught me something and my memories are filled with the time we have shared together. They include my brothers Bob and David, nephews, Darren, Steve and RJ, and friends Don Pettit, Matt Perkins and Mark McCann. And a special thanks goes to the best hunting partner I have ever had or ever hope to have, my son Justin, who also contributed to "A Buck for Justin" — I love you buddy!

I would be remiss if I didn't mention my father, Glenn, who I never got to hunt with but who showed me the pleasures to be had in the great out-of-doors and taught me to shoot when I was just a boy. Thanks dad, I miss you.

Preface

"In intercourse with Nature you are dealing with things at first hand, and you get a rule, a standard, that serves you through life. You are dealing with primal sanities, primal honesties, primal attractions..."
— JOHN BURROUGHS

Remember the old days when shotgun shells were made out of paper? I do! Some of my most prized possessions as a youth were spent hulls that I collected after my dad returned home from a day in the field chasing after pheasants. I kept the hulls in a wooden box, along with other boyhood memorabilia, and frequently took them out to inspect the way they were fashioned and feel the texture of the paper and the brass. I would examine the primer to see if the firing pin struck it in the same place every time. It didn't! I vividly recall the distinctive odor of those shells, the unmistakable combination of burnt gunpowder and paper. There's nothing else quite like it and if I think about it hard enough, I can still smell the fragrance of those shotshells today.

Unfortunately, it took me twenty years to become intimately acquainted with cedar wood arrows. My knowledge of them is a result of my evolution as a hunter, rather than a block placed during the construction of my childhood foundation and even though my time with them has been significantly shorter, cedar shafts hold no less important place in the recesses of my mind than shotshells. The simplicity and beauty of a finely crafted cedar arrow is something even the uninitiated can appreciate. The way the feathers lay perfectly on the rounded shaft, the brilliance and smoothness of the crown dip and subtle markings of the crest. All of this essential finery transitions through the distinctive grain of the wood itself to terminate in the honed sharpness of a simple two bladed broadhead. But again, the best attribute that cedar shafts possess is their aroma. Breaking an arrow, no matter how hard I try to avoid it, has its own reward. Snapping the shaft off just behind the point, as so often happens, brings with it the pungent odor of Port Orford cedar straight from America's northwest coast. I cannot bust an arrow without inhaling the bouquet of the damaged end, as I'm sure every archer has since cedar came into use by arrowsmiths.

Shotshells and Cedar Shafts are the instruments of my pastime, the objects of my affection. Neither a weekend warrior nor a professional sportsman, hunting comprises numerous threads in the fabric of my life. Whether it's been dreaming about adventures to come, enjoying the experience at hand or fondly reliving hunts of bygone days, I don't remember a time when hunting has not been an integral constituent of my existence. At the same time however, I do not profess to own expertise of any kind other than to be someone who has always been willing to take on and master new challenges. As I look around, the tools of my trade surround me from stick bows to snowshoes, canoes with wooden paddles to mountain bikes, and muzzleloading shotguns to cross-country skis. Together they form the manifestation of my adopted philosophy of doing it the hard way. Why go to be one with Nature, expend horsepower, and rely on technology when it is much more gratifying, much more rewarding, to expend human power through bipedal locomotion and utilize simple tools?

This book is a compilation of hunting stories from my time spent wandering fields and forests, swamps and mountains over the past quarter of a century. In that time, I have experienced the thrill of hard earned success, measured in a variety of ways, and the agony of the feet and other such maladies. Decked out in all my camouflaged regalia, I have chased elk up mountains in sweltering heat when swimwear and tanning lotion were more appropriate. I have spent hours sitting on stand in subfreezing temperatures only to learn I was so cold that drawing a bow would be impossible. Longing for a game bird of any kind to take wing, I have walked miles and miles without seeing a feather only to return home to comb burrs out of my dog's wet, matted coat for what seemed like hours.

Even though my experiences are the basis of each story, this book is about, and for, everyman whether young or old, rich or not so rich, man or woman, neophyte or seasoned veteran. In other words, it's for you! It's yours to read and enjoy, to rekindle and be warmed by your own fond memories of adventures past and to dream of, and plan, those yet to come. It's also yours to help you reminisce about times shared with friends and family. These stories are meant to add fuel to the fires that burn within, to motivate you to get out there, enjoy the sporting life, and hopefully take someone along with you to share in the experience. I am optimistic, as well, that it will confirm your need to play the game right and take satisfaction in knowing that you did so.

This is your invitation to throw a log on the fire, sit back, relax and enjoy my outdoor adventures with shotgun and recurve bow. So it is, with a small amount of pride and a large dose of humility that I share with you my tales as a hunter using *Shotshells and Cedar Shafts*.

— Bruce A. Hopkins
Oriskany Falls, NY
2002

CHAPTER 1

Rooster Tales – First Bird

As a kid growing up in central New York in the 60s and 70s, I
remember when the ring-necked pheasant ruled as the bird
hunter's favorite quarry. Not coincidently, this is the same period of
time when pheasant populations peaked in our area, where agriculture
was slowly waning and the landscape was transforming to a more
wooded texture. The first distinct memory I have of pheasant hunting is being allowed to trail along with my dad, who carried an old
Winchester 16 gauge pump gun, and one of the family's dogs to the
crop fields and brush lots surrounding our homestead. On one hunt
in particular, my dad was successful in harvesting one of the more
beautiful things I had ever seen, a mature rooster bird whose tail must
have been at least two feet long.

I recall that the day was very typical of mid-autumn in our part
of the world. Clouds hung thick and low overhead, and the air was
cool and dank. The soil was soft and wet, and water oozed out of
it if you stood in one place very long. Strangely enough, I can't tell

you anything about the taking of the bird itself. I don't remember the flush, the shot or the bird falling to the ground. But what I do remember vividly is catching up to my dad, having him hand me his trophy and asking me to carry it home. Being a young boy, I had all I could do to haul the bird. Its spurs were long, slightly curved and razor sharp and jabbed me in a number of places as I experimented with various ways to carry it. Initially I let it dangle alongside me, first on my right flank then on the left. Then I tried tossing the feathered carcass over my shoulder. Finally, I cradled it in both arms like a football. After struggling with it for quite a while, my dad graciously relieved me of the chore. Now that I look back at it, he probably came to my rescue due to us exiting good bird cover more than with anything else. Since he wasn't wearing a coat or a vest with a game bag, he didn't have a convenient place to stow the cock bird away. As we slogged our way through a spent cornfield toward its low-lying end, I keenly remember a flock of geese taking wing just yards in front of us. They effortlessly lifted toward the heavens and my head was swimming in the grandeur of the afternoon that I had just shared with my father.

It was a few years later, after tagging along with dad on a number of occasions and shortly after his unexpected death, that I found myself anxiously waiting for the moment that I could place my first cock bird in my hunting vest. I ached for the presence of my dad but that was not to be. Fortunately though, he had instilled a desire to hunt in both of my older brothers, and I now counted on them to take me to the fields to chase the wily pheasant. David, who I've always referred to as my "younger, older brother" was the first to take me. We hunted over a crossbreed dog named Trudy, which was probably more setter than anything else. She was one of several dogs we had around the house when I was growing up. Trudy and the others were pets first, hunting dogs second. Our family didn't spend much time training our mutts other than to take them to the field repeatedly and let Mother Nature guide them in a game instilled deep within from generations past. A trained setter will point a bird but I never saw Trudy point anything. We would watch her work the cover and when she got wind of a bird, she'd get low to the ground and her tail would wag as if in hyper drive. More often than not if the bird was a hen, it would sit tight and take flight in short order. But if the bird was a rooster, it usually tried to run off. With Trudy on its trail, you'd better have your track boots on in order to keep up. Looking back, it sometimes was comical. Trudy would find a bird and start working it. Then she'd take off and knowing that we'd better stay with her, we'd take off after her. She would slow down and we'd be sure that a bird was about to burst from the cover, so each of us would try to figure out the best position to be in if the bird got up. After a while she'd stop, double back and take off again. And we would do the same. Start, then stop, over and over — sometimes a bird would flush, other times not. This to me was pheasant hunting and when these chases resulted in a rooster taking flight, it was as exhilarating as anything could be.

Those were also the days of the old TV show *The American Sportsman* hosted by Curt Gowdy. Oh, how I loved that show. I would sit and watch Curt with the star of the week chasing game all over the world and imagine myself striding through the fields alongside them. When they would televise pheasant hunting, they'd put up bird after bird and often take their limit home with them. This was not the case in my formative years of pheasant hunting. Even though it was the peak of the pheasant population in our "neck of

the woods," we didn't live in South Dakota! We'd consider ourselves fortunate if we put a rooster up within gun range in the
course of a morning or afternoon hunt. After numerous trips afield
with my older brothers, before being old enough to tote a gun
myself, I was more than ready to experience the thrill of victory.

I was fourteen when my first season finally rolled along. Bird
hunting would be an endeavor to be pursued after school and on
weekends. It was on one of those afternoon hunts that Dave and I found
ourselves on the Scudder place about a mile from our home, an area
that had consistently held birds in the past. Dave carried an Ithaca Sweet
16, which ejected spent shells from the bottom, a must for him since
he shoots a gun left handed. Evidently finding a gun for a lefty wasn't
as easy in those days as it is today. I was armed with a WesternField
bolt-action 20 gauge which dad had purchased for me from the
Montgomery Ward store in town a couple of years earlier. We'd been
hunting for quite a while with little to show for it. Trudy was slowing down and I was working up a pretty good sweat fighting through
scrub fields, hedgerows and pursuing the dog on quickened chases that
resulted in nothing more than deflated expectations.

As the canvas of the western sky began to be painted in orange
and yellow hues by the setting sun, we were fast approaching a corner brush lot just off a cut cornfield. I call it a brush lot but in actuality, it wasn't all that brushy. It was mostly covered with dried up
grasses, forbs and goldenrod, decent bird habitat for our area. Trudy
was happily working the cover zigzagging out in front of us, like all
good bird dogs do, when a scent stream turned her up the hill. Dave
was on my right and we took off after the dog huffing and puffing
as we charged upslope. Unlike many previous pursuits, this one was
relatively short. Trudy crashed into the junk and a rooster bird

exploded straight up gaining altitude in a hurry. Brotherly love only goes so far so I wasn't sure if Dave would hold off or go ahead and dump that bird right in front of me. Knowing I only had one good shot given the bolt-action nature of my gun, I wanted to make sure it was a good one. I got up on the bird quickly but then took my time "aiming" the gun to make an accurate shot. I was also half listening for a discharge from the gun to my right, but it never came. Finally, I yanked the trigger and the bird's quickening wing beats fluttered, and then stopped all together as the bird tumbled to earth with a thud. I whooped and hollered as I stood over my first cock pheasant.

As I picked the bird up it dawned on me that it didn't have the heft of the pheasant my dad shot years ago. It was a young bird, his tail barely a foot long, and absent any spurs capable of scratching me. But it still was a trophy of immeasurable importance. Fumbling to put the bird in my vest, Dave came over to help me out and asked why it took so long for me to shoot. "I just wanted to be sure of the shot," was my only reply. The weight of the bird's mass in my game bag was a pleasing feeling as we turned toward home. We hunted our way there with no further action but I couldn't have cared less given the events of the day. The only thing that would have made the moment better would've been if dad were there with us, with Curt along just for fun. Oh, the things that our dreams are made of. We arrived at the house when the leaden sky was nearly devoid of light, as a skein of geese coursed its way south. As I became mesmerized by their methodical wing beats, I knew in my heart that dad was watching and nodding in approval of me taking my first bird.

CHAPTER 2

Whack, Thunk, Whap

The transition from what I call modern day archery to traditional bowhunting takes a lot more effort than just purchasing or building a stick bow then learning how to shoot it. Although that's just the way I initially attempted my transformation, some years ago, with a little help from a newfound friend who was skilled in the ways of two sticks and a string. Waiting for the delivery of my Robertson recurve bow, like a kid yearns for Christmas, was an excruciating experience. When it finally arrived, it became one of my most prized possessions. But unlike a new toy on Christmas morning, it took the passage of several days for me to string it up and shoot it due to my inexperience with traditional equipment. I had waited until my mentor, Greg Haskell, inventor of Skyline camouflage, and I could get together and go through all the basics of stringing and tuning a recurve bow before beginning my journey into the world of traditional bowhunting. There was no question that I was a greenhorn, but due to G. Fred Asbell's book, *Instinctive*

Shooting, which had recently been published, I was not ignorant. Reading Fred's book from cover to cover, highlighting various excerpts that I felt essential to my successful mastery of the instinctive shooting style, I had a good start at becoming an instinctive stick bow shooter.

From that point in late spring until opening day of bow season, I spent many hours shooting my bow daily, habituating my mind and muscles to shoot my Robertson smoothly and accurately. Arrow after arrow was shot at very close range making sure both eyes were open, knees were bent and an intense focus was given to the spot I intended to hit. Fortunately for me, I lived in the middle of rural New York state so I could literally step out my back door and start "stump shooting" at all sorts of targets, from goldenrod galls to rotten stumps, to leaves lying on the forest floor. This enabled me to practice at varying distances, shooting uphill and down; rehearsing various scenarios that I hoped would, some day, become reality. By the time opening morning rolled around I felt very confident in my ability to shoot the bow. However, as I would come to find out, shooting a recurve and hunting with it are two entirely different things.

It was early in the bow season when I headed to my favorite treestand to spend the afternoon under clear blue autumn skies with a nip in the air that felt just about right. This was my fifth trip afield in the young season, which had been somewhat uneventful to that point. Numerous does and fawns had presented potential opportunities but I was looking for something with antlers atop its head. Not big ones mind you; but right, wrong or indifferent, I wanted my first traditional harvest to have "horns." I had seen several bucks, none of which had presented me with what I would call a good shot. However, this hunt would be different. The last hour of the day was winding down when a little brush buck made his way toward my stand. He had come in perfectly, totally unsuspecting of my presence, easing through the woods headed for some predetermined yet undisclosed destination. The buck paid no attention to the handful of scrapes that appeared every fall in this corner woods. Traditional bowhunting requires up-close and personal contact with your intended quarry and this young buck was providing me with just that as he approached to within ten yards. Unfortunately, he came in head on and didn't present me with a good angle until he was just about underneath my stand.

I'd successfully hunted this location before but I was now positioned in a different tree, which I felt provided me with even more possibilities than I had in the past: It was quite a bit bigger and straighter and provided a better background to break up my Lincolnesque silhouette. A Loc-On stand had been erected well in advance of the season and I conservatively trimmed shooting lanes out to twenty-five yards or so; although that kind of distance wasn't required since this buck was no more than five or six steps away when he finally presented me with a nice quartering shot. Doing my best to concentrate on the sweet spot behind his shoulder, I slowly raised and drew my bow. The instant the middle finger of my right hand hit the corner of my mouth the bowstring slipped away, releasing the arrow toward my intended target. I don't think the arrow had even cleared the bow when the solemn silence of the north woods was shattered with a thunderous WHACK!

Regrettably, I had chosen not to cut a sapling growing next to my stand tree that I felt, at one time, presented few problems for any potential shot I might have. I was mistaken. I had cut several branches off that tree but my top limb struck the trunk of the sapling solidly due to the canting of the bow. The arrow errantly flew over the startled buck's back causing him to bolt off. He tore out of there in a big hurry, probably ending up somewhere in the next township! After inspecting my bow to ensure that no permanent damage had been done, I began repairing my shaken confidence knowing that I had just screwed up big time. Before I left the woods that evening, I removed a brush saw from my fanny pack and cut the sapling off well below my treestand. My initiation into the world of traditional bowhunting was not a pleasant one!

I continued to hunt hard for a couple of more weeks seeing numerous deer but with no luck at getting a good shot at a buck. The rut was fast approaching and I knew, deep down inside, that I would get another chance. Finally, it looked as though I would get a break on an early November afternoon in the same stand where I had my previous encounter. This buck, another rag-horn, came in from the big woods, with his nose to the ground and circled around to a scrape that was off to my left. He stopped momentarily to paw at the scrape and check the ever-present overhanging branch. As it happens more often than not, his rump was pointed directly at me. Obviously, I had no shot, so I held my bow with slight tension on the string prepared to draw and shoot if the buck offered a better shooting angle. Depending on the season, local deer population, weather, my schedule and mental attitude, I can pretty much count on at least one good opportunity to take a buck in any given year. Most years, I can be confident in getting a couple of good cracks at it if necessary. So, three weeks into my first traditional season, chance number two was about to present itself and this time there was no rogue sapling to mess things up!

As the buck finished his requisite duties at the scrape, he turned and headed down a well-used trail that would put him broadside at fifteen yards or so. There was an old, decaying log across the trail the buck would have to step over and it was on the lower side of that log that I would have a clear shot at him. So I timed my draw to coincide with the moment he cleared the log. My draw and anchor were perfect. My release, smooth as could be. However, I was so focused on the deer getting over the log and stepping into my only good shooting lane that I had completely ignored the need to pick a spot. THUNK! This time the arrow got off cleanly and flew perfectly, perfectly over the deer's back, auguring itself into the gold-carpeted forest floor. Fred would not be pleased with me. Thankfully, I didn't need to inspect my bow after the shot and due to the fact that there were no loud noises emanating from the vicinity of my stand, the deer trotted away, totally unaware of my attempt to fill the freezer with his carcass.

It's at times like this that one starts to question whether they have made a bad choice, and at that time and place, I was no exception as I wondered whether this traditional thing was going to be doable. I reminded myself that anything worth doing is often difficult. As Howard Hill said, "It's hunting the hard way." And I knew, full well, that I chose to do this not only because it would be challenging, and therefore very satisfying, but also because of the distinct advantages traditional bowhunting offers over modern day archery, namely simplicity. Even though I was frustrated by my feeble attempts at taking my first deer with traditional gear, I knew it was just a matter of bringing all the simplicity together at one time and making it work for me. After all, it really is just a matter of picking a spot, drawing the bow and letting go! So I continued to hunt hard.

Even though I was hunting numerous stands, the corner wood-lot continued to hold deer and was the one area I could count on. With just a week remaining in the season, it was there I found myself yet again. I had tried to hunt that morning at a different location but a strong line of thunderstorms was moving through and I didn't feel like getting soaked, let alone sit in a metal treestand fifteen feet up in the air with lightning in the vicinity. Therefore, I bided my time, waiting for the evening hunt as the season marched onward. The front, however, greatly benefited my late day outing by turning the winds in my favor and I was able to avail myself of my most productive stand.

Mid-afternoon found me climbing into my perch, plenty early I felt, and taking a seat to wait for prime time when I would stand upright for that last magical hour of daylight. Twenty minutes later, I was surprised to spy a small seven pointer coming in from the direction of an adjacent meadow. He was steadily walking from left to right. Startled, I dang near jumped to my feet to ready myself for the impending shot. Gathering my senses, I eased up as the deer stopped broadside at about twenty yards. Reaching my apex I quickly realized that there was a hemlock bough obstructing my view of, and thus my shot at, the vital area of the buck. Having no other option, I slowly crouched down on my haunches in order to get a clear shot at the deer. Fortuitously, he cooperated by staring straight ahead through the woods at either something or nothing. I knew not which, nor did I care! Due to a lack of proper shooting form, and with potential obstacles between the deer and me, I was forced to cant my bow to a nearly horizontal attitude, a position that is seldom used with today's technology-driven archery tackle. This time the simple act of picking a spot, drawing the bow and letting go came together perfectly. WHAP! The arrow found its mark. Because of my somewhat unorthodox shooting stance, the arrow went a little higher than intended with the result being a nonexistent trailing job as the deer literally fell in its tracks.

I had done it! I had made the switch. And a feeling of extreme satisfaction overwhelmed me as I placed my bow and arrows beside the buck and snapped a few pictures for my hunting album. All the practice had paid off and I found it in myself to hang in there and keep trying even though reverting back to wheels and cables would have been an easy thing to do. Success is sweetest when it comes the hard way. Hopefully in the future though, I won't always need three words to sum up my traditional bowhunting experiences.

CHAPTER 3

Quick Draw McGraw

Hunting ruffed grouse is an endeavor that stands alone in my mind when it comes to wingshooting. It's much the same no matter where you go and there aren't a half a dozen techniques to master like there are when chasing ducks or pheasants. I'm not sure that anyone is necessarily born to be a grouse hunter but I'm confident that no one just falls into being one either, especially a good one. I don't want to give the impression that I am now, or ever was, a great grouse hunter but I think that in my prime I could hold my own with just about anyone. Just to make things clear, I'm not speaking to the history of the sport, selection of the best shoulder arms or which dogs to use in the pursuit of the "king of game birds." What I am talking about is being able to find good cover, locate birds and bring them to hand. And in order to do this con-sistently, a person needs to hone their skills, over a period of years, and actually evolve into an effective grouse hunter.

Let's face it: The skill you really need is being able to hit the gosh-darned things. And this is not an easy task given that grouse do very little in the way of advertising their existence, let alone their location. They seek out the thickest, thorniest places to cloister themselves away in and when discovered, explode to flight, careening through limbs, leaves, vines and boughs with the maneuverability of an F-16. Frankly, all this may lead one to the conclusion that they make for a very challenging target! Over the years, I have chased partridge with dozens of folks. Some of them were adept at putting them in their game bags, others not so but all of them agree that there isn't a much more difficult target around. In addition, consider this, I enjoy reading about hunting of all kinds, frequently view outdoor shows on television and own quite a collection of videos on the subject. There are literally scores of articles, books, shows and tapes in the marketplace on ducks, geese, turkeys, pheasants and quail but there are precious few on ruffed grouse. Why? Because it's tough hunting, but if you put in the time, you can fashion yourself into a fair, if not a good, grouse marksman.

After spending innumerable hours in the grouse woods, I have developed what I call the "Quick Draw McGraw" method of hunting partridge. Just to make things clear, I am not referring to the mechanics of good shooting form here. What I am pointing out is how to go about being able to shoot lightning fast and accurately. I call it this because a friend of mine, twenty plus years ago, inquired whether I was some kind of "Quick Draw McGraw," referring to the mid 1960s cartoon character, upon my downing of a grouse, which I'll get to in a moment. This methodology involves three very important ingredients: attitude, preparation and visualization.

"Attitude is everything," according to the old adage. If you're going out for a nice walk in the woods that's one thing, but if your objective is to put the breast meat from a brace of grouse on the dinner table, that's quite another. The successful grouse hunting attitude is being patient, yet aggressive, and knowing, deep down in your gut, that every covert you encounter holds at least one bird. Being surprised by a partridge when it flushes requires you to go through a thought process in order to put everything in motion to harvest that bird. If, on the other hand, you knew that a grouse was going to take wing, everything else becomes instinctual, thus increasing the odds that you will add it to the game bag.

To illustrate this point I will refer back to my experience, over two decades ago, with my old friend Mark. It was a gorgeous October day, with most of autumn's leafy jewels still on the trees, when we had decided to hunt some property near his home. I had never stepped foot on the place but Mark had indicated that the old farm held some grouse. It also had a pond on the backside of the property where wood ducks were known to loaf away the day. We hunted some decent cover for an hour or so without seeing much when we came to a right-of-way that led back to the pond. Mark wanted to see if we could jump shoot a duck or two and recommended walking the right-of-way as a means to quietly sneak in on them. We were still in good grouse habitat so my mind remained focused on that fact, even though I was also carrying on a casual, albeit quiet, conversation with Mark as we furtively tiptoed down the path. Now this right-of-way had fallen off the maintenance schedule and was in the process of reverting to a more forested condition. I would generously say that it was no more than twelve to fifteen feet wide. My springer spaniel, Gina, was working the cover to our left as we walked side by side down the path. Somewhere in between the talk about cars and girls, a grouse exploded from the edge of the thicket on our right and no more than ten to fifteen yards out in front of us. The bird could have gone right, but instead flew to the left and away from us. I reacted instantly to the bird and dropped it at the opposite edge of the roadway with an ounce and a quarter of 7½s before Mark had even shouldered his gun. He could not believe that I had raised my gun, tracked the target, slapped the trigger and downed the bird that fast, thus the query regarding "Quick Draw McGraw."

So why was it that I was able to "out draw" Mark and harvest that partridge? I maintain that it was all about attitude. We hadn't seen a grouse in our first hour of hunting. I'm sure a little bit of disappointment, if not doubt, was creeping into Mark's consciousness

as he had told me that this was a pretty good covert. Second, Mark had gone from grouse mode to duck mode. He was thinking about how many and what type of ducks might be sitting on that pond rather than focusing on the possibility that there might be a grouse waiting around the next bend. Last, Mark and I were carefree, single young guys back then and talk of hotrods, and especially young ladies, was more than of casual interest to both of us. But at that time and place, I think I was a little more interested in fanned tails than he was. My entire mind was focused on the reality, not the possibility that a bird would take off at any moment. It did and the facts speak for themselves.

As most people know, one of the Boy Scout's mottos is "Be prepared" and as many successful folks have said down through the ages, "Preparation is everything." This holds true with grouse hunting as it does with most things. I could hone in on a lot of things relative to being prepared when coursing after partridge, including the correct apparel, hunting good country, and choosing the right firearms and ammo. But when I talk about being prepared, I'm focusing on endowing oneself mentally and physically for the rise of the next grouse, because there always is a next one (there's that attitude again). Whether you're hunting alone or with a companion or two, with a dog or without, you must constantly be prepared for action in order to react in a quick, decisive and effective manner. I have strode through grouse thickets with numerous people who have not been, in any way, ready for the eventuality of a grouse getting up within range of their gun.

So, what is being prepared all about? First, I've never seen anyone who effectively harvests birds; walk through the fields and forests without having their gun "primed" for action. Preparing to shoot is having both hands on your gun in good shooting position with your finger at the ready to click off the safety and reach for the trigger. Your gun cannot be in one hand at your side, cradled in your arms or God forbid, up over your shoulder if you expect to bring it to point and aim in the time it takes to get at least one good shot off at a grouse. It must be in "ready mode" to come to your shoulder, while tracking the bird and firing the instant you have a good, safe shot. The second aspect of being prepared is to have a strategy about how you'll hunt a specific piece of cover. Grouse inhabit some thick places. If you can hunt an edge, a right-of-way or some other relatively clear space where grouse may traverse the sky, by all means do it! This, however, is most often not the case and if you want to maximize the number of shot opportunities you get, you're going to have to tackle cover that may initially look impenetrable. Fortunately, the thick stuff is rarely homogeneously thick. There are usually small clearings and lanes within it that provide you with enough room to get your gun up and swing with your target. Here's where a lot of folks could improve their grouse hunting success. My approach to this situation is busting through the junk as quickly as possible and when in the clear stop, wait and listen. I don't do this aimlessly though: I look ahead and try to imagine where my opportunities lie and zigzag my way to the openings where I can have at least a chance at any bird that might get up. Before moving to the next shooting window, I always feign my departure; sometimes I even vocalize a flushing noise to see if I can get a bird to go out. This strategy has yielded me great success over the years and once practiced, it becomes the natural manner in which you hunt.

Several years ago a colleague of mine named Matt, asked if I might be interested in hunting his family's farm in southwestern

New York State. Always looking for new hills to climb, I graciously accepted. We'd been hunting a brushy hillside, without a dog, and had several birds go up without any shooting. As we worked our way in each other's direction, in order to strategize what to do next, we headed up a steep slope toward an opening in the woods. We ended up walking side by side, as we approached an old logging road. After disentangling myself from the brush and briars, I instinctively stopped at the edge of the small clearing. Matt paused, with gun at his side, and then took a couple of steps when a grouse exploded out from the cover just a few feet away. Standing there, with gun at "half draw," I smoothly came up into firing position and knocked the bird down as it crossed the woods opening. Again, my hunting companion was amazed. He hadn't even gotten his gun up to shoot let alone pull the trigger. But by virtue of the fact that I was in the clear, gun at ready and fixed to shoot, the bird was a relatively easy target. It was also the biggest grouse I had ever harvested, which hadn't hurt my chances any.

If you're a sports fan, you've probably seen a number of athletes close their eyes and visualize what they were about to do. The skier does it before heading down the mountain, the biker before pedaling off down the road and the hurdler before getting into the blocks. I feel that the ability to visualize something either before or as it happens is necessary in order to be a successful grouse hunter and in grouse hunting, the visualizing needs to be done with both eyes open. Given that the bulk of partridge country doesn't lend itself to long, clear shots, many opportunities are lost when a branch, bough or tree trunk blocks your line of sight to a bird. Grouse are amazing fliers and can twist and turn through almost any type of cover. Once a bird takes to flight, you have two to three seconds to react and pull the trigger. Maybe! Two or three seconds isn't that long relative to the hours spent on any given outing. Think about it: In the time it takes you to read this sentence, the bird is gone. And in that time, you may or may not have a good open shot and, more likely than not, you're going to have to shoot through thick cover to kill that bird. I can't begin to count the number of birds I've harvested that I couldn't actually see at the report of the gun. But due to my ability to visualize the flight path of the bird and track its apparent course, I have bagged plenty of birds that were obscured at the time I yanked the trigger.

My nephew, Darren, and I have hunted partridge together dozens of times and we have learned to hunt as a team with and without canine assistance. We took a break from pursuing whitetails with sticks and strings a few years back to see if we could scrape up a grouse or two off of an old farm that we had hunted numerous times. It was a warm, dry autumn day — one of those days that you'd probably be better off raking leaves than hunting. However, we'd rather hunt than rake so we were out there busting through the brush. We had hunted hard for quite a while when we decided to stop for the day and get a cold drink. Walking along an old tractor path through a wild apple orchard, we reminisced about all the grouse that we had taken off the farm. My dog was wearing down in the heat but she was still checking out most of the nooks and crannies within shotgun range. Suddenly, a grouse exploded out of the cover, going from right to left out in front of me. Due to my "Quick Draw McGraw" approach to grouse hunting, my mind and body were prepared for the opportunity. As I brought the gun up, the grouse flew behind a small hemlock grove. Visualizing his flight path, my gun followed suit and the next thing I knew, I had instinctively pulled the trigger sending hemlock needles into a great, green explosion. The grouse never exited from behind the swaying boughs. Before I knew it, the dog entered the grove and emerged with the bird softly secured in her mouth. Darren just looked at me, shook his head in disbelief, and asked, "How in the heck did you do that?" I replied, "Just a little something I learned while watching Saturday morning cartoons."

CHAPTER 4

The Bulls of Wolf Lake

The hunt was ending in much the same way it started, with our hunting party standing on a gravel airstrip nearly one thousand miles north of Montreal. It was cloudy, cool, and windy with light rain falling — the same conditions we experienced as we arrived at camp a week earlier. That day was filled with anticipation as the start of our five-day Quebec-Labrador caribou hunt began. We were hunting with Ungava Adventures at their Wolf Lake camp, a very comfortable outpost consisting of wooden cabins, a mess hall, and a meat house nestled on a small bay of Wolf Lake some forty miles southwest of Kuujjuaq (Fort Chimo), Canada. Our flight in aboard a twin Otter, however, put a lid on our anticipation as we flew over miles of treeless tundra seeing very few caribou. Upon reaching our destination, we learned that the previous group had to be flown to outlying camps in order to get into the thick of the caribou migration. The remainder of that first day had us putting our gear together, shooting a few arrows, and glassing the desolate countryside in hopes of seeing a caribou, all the while, wondering what our fate might be.

Darren, a somewhat younger, more spirited version of me, would be my hunting partner for the week. We were in camp with nine other hunters; six were toting smoke poles for the weeklong adventure. The balance of the group were bowhunters, one shooting a compound, one a longbow, and our party, including Darren's high school buddy, Dave Pfeiffer, shooting recurves. Caribou hunting is great if you're not an early riser. There is no need to get up well before dawn to effectively hunt the nomads of the north. The routine is much more relaxed than that: get up and dressed in the early morning light, eat a leisurely breakfast, and head out to the wide open spaces in search of white-maned bulls. It didn't take long for me to realize that this hunt was not going to be the type that I had read so much about, the kind that you're dropped off at a spot on a lake or river where caribou tend to cross. This was a hunt where we would put some miles on our boot bottoms, spotting and stalking what game we could find.

We departed camp the first morning by boat and cruised down the length of Wolf Lake, glassing as we went. Immediately we realized that a profound change had occurred overnight. The previous day there were no caribou to be found anywhere. As we headed down the lake, though, we could see massive antlers silhouetted against the low-hanging, gray sky on the ridges to the south of us. Having spotted a nice bull close to shore, we put the boat in and the hunt was on.

Caribou walk much faster than I thought and all we could do is watch as that first bull just ambled away. We then headed toward a small river valley when I spotted antlers bobbing below the crest of a small hill. After a short stalk over the quiet moss and lichen-covered ground, I worked myself into position for a thirty-yard shot. Whether it was due to the distance, rush of adrenalin, or size of the bull I'll never know, but my arrow sailed harmlessly over his back. He scooted off, not like a whitetail, but more like a puppy that's just been scolded; he ran about twenty yards, stopped, looked back then turned and walked away. He was a big bull too, good tops and tremendous bottoms, with huge double shovels. For the balance of that first day, Darren, our guide Tommy and I stalked, headed off, and even tried to herd countless numbers of caribou. Late in the afternoon, we got separated and ended up hunting on our own. We had spotted hundreds of caribou throughout the day; many of them huge bulls, especially compared to the whitetails that I've chased around the woodlots back home in New York.

Upon our arrival back at camp that evening, we landed the boat on the beach in front of numerous caribou antlers and capes that had been collected throughout the day. I came back empty handed but the riflemen were very successful: six hunters, eleven bulls. We bowhunters also had some success. Of the five of us, three arrowed nice bulls, including Darren who shot one while we were going in different directions. However, his caribou ended up expiring in a small lake, a common event in this corner of the globe, and had to be retrieved the next morning. With the cold water, and air temperatures dipping into the thirties, the bull would be fine. Having missed a good bull earlier in the day was bad enough but seeing all the beautiful trophies displayed before me was somewhat hard to swallow. That night I lay awake wondering what I could do to increase my chances during the remainder of my hunt. There certainly wasn't a place for a treestand in this country.

The next morning brought with it an approaching storm front. It was cool and breezy as we pushed off from shore. After coming out of the small bay, where our camp was situated, we started down the lake. We immediately saw a band of caribou feeding among some dwarf spruce trees and brush and pulled into shore ahead of them. My first thought: Be aggressive! I'm not a great stalker but in order to have any luck I felt that I just had to go for it and not pussyfoot around. The caribou were quartering away from the lake with the wind perpendicular to their line of travel and toward the water, a perfect set-up. There was also some cover, a rare commodity in the tundra, to help conceal my six foot four inch frame. Much of the herd, walking at a steady pace into the wind, got by me. However, I could see one bull out in front of me, his head down, feeding.

I crouched and crawled more than one hundred yards only to run out of screening vegetation. The bull was fifty yards away, but still more interested in gorging himself than moving on. Looking over the situation, I decided to hustle though the football field-wide opening between us while his muzzle was still buried in his breakfast. I made it easily and crept in for a shot only to have the bull lift his head and start walking toward me and to my left. He stopped even with me twenty yards away, but the same brush that helped me get within range now obscured his vitals. The old boy then turned and walked completely around me to my right, maintaining a constant distance. My heart was pounding, and I was consciously taking deep breaths to calm my nerves. I picked an opening and waited for him to step into it. As he did, he walked up onto a little hummock giving me a clear shot. My sixty pound Robertson Stykbow came back and I instantaneously released my Zwickey Eskimo tipped cedar shaft. The shot was good and the big bull trotted off. He went down in short order and it was time to take a big sigh of relief, enjoy the moment, and then get to the work at hand. In our haste to get out of the boat, all of our still-cameras were left behind; fortunately though, Darren got some nice video. We packed out the antlers, cape and meat reflecting on our good fortune as we began to thoroughly fall in love with caribou hunting.

Later the video proved very interesting. Darren not only got some good footage of my trophy bull, but had videotaped the stalk and subsequent errant shot I had made the day before. While viewing it back in the comfort of my living room several weeks later, I realized that the bull I harvested was the same one I had missed the first morning of the hunt. What are the chances of that?

By the end of the second day, all the bowhunters in camp had taken respectable bull caribou. Now we had the remainder of the week to concentrate on filling our second tags. Darren got the first opportunity. Due to extremely high winds, we headed out of camp on foot that third day. We hadn't gone half a mile when we spotted three bulls bedded down along the shoreline of Wolf Lake. Since I had the last stalk, I told Darren to go for it. It was going to be tough, there was a lot of real estate between us and the bulls, no cover, and a fickle wind. But Darren's a better stalker than I am and no more did the words get out of my mouth and he was on his way. I watched through my binoculars as the entire event unfolded before my eyes. Darren belly crawled for several hundred yards and worked his way to within spitting distance of the biggest bull. Just as he was preparing to pull up and shoot, a nearby cow spotted him and spooked. The bull got up in an instant and Darren made a hard quartering away shot. Unbelievably, this bull too wound up succumbing in the lake. At that point, Darren had earned a new nick-name — "Lake 'Em." The rest of that day edified me in the ways of caribou. Where there were hundreds of them two days before, that third day produced next to nothing. After taking care of Darren's trophy, we hiked miles only to see a couple of small bulls and a few cows with calves.

Since Darren had tagged out, I continued hunting on my own. The next to last day of our far north adventure brought sightings of several bulls and a couple of blown stalks, including a second clean miss. I went into the last day of the hunt more than satisfied with our experience. Another caribou would be great but certainly wouldn't make the hunt a success; that had already been accomplished. As I prepared for my last traipse through the tundra, I remembered to clean and sharpen the arrow that I took my first bull with. I told Darren and Dave I intended to take my next caribou with that very same arrow. They both laughed and told me I was a cheap SOB.

Tommy and I took off early that last morning. He wanted to get back by midday in order to prepare our meat and racks for the trip home. As we journeyed down the lake, we spied a large bull on a bluff overlooking the north shoreline. We decided he was a good one, went past him, and pulled into a small inlet on the north side of the lake. I carefully traversed up the slope, using a three point stalking method, not knowing exactly where he was. We found him bedded with several cows, calves, and another bull. Almost immediately, a cow and the smaller bull got up and fed their way below me; I let them pass. The bigger bull had also gotten up and started grazing on the ridge above me. I slinked up the moss-covered rocks to within comfortable bow range of my intended target. He was feeding, head down, and quartering away, another ideal opportunity. Making sure to knock the same arrow that I used to take my first bull, I reminded myself to concentrate and pick a spot. I then eased up on both knees and shot. The cedar shaft found its mark and my weeklong caribou hunt was over. Two mature caribou bulls harvested with one arrow: I guess I am cheap and maybe a little lucky, too!

Overall, the eleven hunters in camp took twenty-two bulls and a black bear. Easy hunting? No way! But there were plenty of animals, which obviously increase your odds and keep your spirits and energy high. You're always confident that there will be a bull over the next ridge. And at Wolf Lake, there are a lot of ridges, and during our visit, there were a lot of bulls. As we flew out in the wind and rain, I glanced down to recognize the bluff overlooking the lake where my hunt had ended. A great feeling overwhelmed me as my mind flashed back to the experience that I had just had. At the same time wondering when I might return, once again, to stalk the bulls of Wolf Lake.

CHAPTER 5

Goose Egg

We had vacillated back and forth the night before whether to go hunting or not, then once it was decided we would, we hemmed and hawed as to what we would hunt. It had been a long week and I was tuckered out, so grouse hunting sounded good to me. I could sleep in a little and still get out and have a chance at a bird or two. But the weather felt more like duck hunting and Darren talked me into getting up earlier than I thought I could. Hell, looking back at it now, almost twenty years later, I didn't even know what tired was then. Staying up half the night, for many a good reason, and then getting up before the sun rose was almost a routine. Now, a solid eight hours of sleep a night is essential, except for pursuing certain activities including hunting the peak of the rut and other such matters. Youth is a terrible thing to waste on the young!

My alarm startled me out of a perfectly good sleep at 4:30 a.m. and I almost crept back down underneath the covers and ignored it. But I didn't. Fortunately, I don't require a lot of preparation time in the morning. I can skip food, and coffee has never been a necessity with me; that time of day is too early to eat and drink, and after throwing on a few warm clothes, I headed out to meet Darren. In those days, my sister lived right down the road and Darren was still staying at home, so the truck hadn't even started to get warm when I pulled into the driveway to pick him up. He threw his gun and waders into the bed of the truck, eased the cap door closed and hopped in. The decoys had already been stowed in the back, fourteen in number, which included four drake mallards, four hen mallards, four black ducks and two geese. Darren and I had actually bought them together at the start of our duck hunting endeavors. Our G & Hs were some of our most prized possessions, along with the homemade anchor lines, which I dyed myself; hardware; lead anchors and a decoy bag. The outfit cost us more than a hundred bucks and in those days, that was a lot of money for two kids.

The old Biddlecum place was our destination and fortunately, it was only a couple of miles away and we had permission to hunt a small pond located on the property. It wasn't the greatest duck hunting to be had, but it was convenient, adjacent to an extensive wetland ecosystem comprised of wooded swamps, an oxbow creek, and a few open marshes. We had a minimalist blind built on the north shore of the pond that consisted of nothing more than brush cuttings stuck into the mud and two pails used as stools. Facing south, with thick woods at our backs, we could see a fair amount of countryside to the west and south, a little less to the east. Ducks could and did come in from any direction, so scanning the sky from horizon to horizon was an absolute must.

After pulling the truck off the road, Darren and I headed to the tailgate to struggle with the job of yanking on our waders. It was dark, the waders were cold and I was prepared to deal with my suspenders, which always seemed to get knotted up. However, on that particular day, everything went smoothly. With guns in hand and decoys hoisted on our backs, we headed down toward the pond. Walking through a small field we both finally realized that there wasn't the slightest breeze in the air. The atmosphere just hung there, cool, calm and damp. This of course did not bode well for duck hunting but what do you do? All you can do is carry on, hoping against all odds that the hunting gods will smile down on you and provide a little action.

After reaching the pond, the ritual of putting out the decoys was the first task at hand. I always had a lot of anxiety over this stratagem: I wasn't an expert in the ways of waterfowl and Darren always had something different in mind than I did. Frankly, except for a few important details, I think the entire hubbub about setting decoys is a tempest in a teapot. Just like real estate, I think duck hunting is more about location than what configuration the blocks are laid out in. With only two of us hunting, we finally agreed on a straight forward spread with eight duck decoys to the west and six to the east paralleling the shore, with a hole right out in front of us. As an afterthought, our two confidence decoys, floating geese, were placed alone at the far east end of the pond. Since there was no wind to set up for, we figured that the layout that we ended up with was just as good as any. In order to liven things up a bit, we waded around the blocks to muddy up the water, then headed to shore.

Settling down on our buckets, guns across our laps, we waited for the appointed hour to arrive when we could at least hope for a little shooting. Sitting in the dark, we tried to raise the other's hopes but with no wind, both of us knew it might be a long morning. Even when conditions weren't conducive to the hunt we usually stuck it out for at least a couple of hours. Besides, what else was there to do? The rest of the world wasn't awake, going back to bed was never an option and football games were hours away. The sky was obscured with cloud cover and even though it was getting lighter, it wasn't getting much brighter. This day was going from jet black to dark gray and back again and that was it. After checking our watches for the umpteenth time, legal shooting light had finally arrived. As expected, it wasn't marked by action of any kind, as we had solemnly predicted. With the passing of each minute, our expectations sank lower and lower, because if there aren't ducks in the air early, then later isn't going to be any better. At one point in the monotony, we did see a duck or two flying high and fast but our little waterhole was not their intended destination.

The day was about as bright as it was going to get and we scanned the sky so intently that both of us started to see things. Every blip in the air gained a lot of scrutiny as it passed by. Morning doves and blackbirds started to look like woodies and teal. Then, off to the west, a faint sound floated into our consciousness, a steady rhythm growing closer and closer. Searching the gray blanket of clouds, we couldn't pick them out at first but we knew that they were there. Were they up high or down low? We couldn't tell but one thing was certain: They were headed in our direction as the honking grew louder and louder. Canada geese are, to me, some of the most graceful, dignified, majestic creatures on earth. They are smart, vigilant and mate for life. While they're certainly not beautiful in the same way a wood duck is, their beauty is the essence of simplicity and grace. Even though I think so highly of the bird, I had never really hunted them specifically. They have been nothing more than an incidental harvest while pursuing their smaller cousins.

Straining our eyes, we started to pick them out of the murky haze that engulfed them, about a dozen birds flying in a loose formation just over the treetops. Neither Darren nor I had a goose call with us, not that we really thought it would do any good. We had a dozen puddle duck and two goose decoys dead still in the water. And there was no way that this small flock of wary geese would give it a first look let alone a second. Hunkering down as low as we could get, we noticed a truck on the road to the south of us slowing down, and then stopping. The truck was several hundred yards away, but we could see the window go down and someone peering through binoculars in our direction. Darren spoke up, realizing that the truck belonged to his old man. Jack had been married to my sister for quite a while and was the father of my sister's three boys, with Darren being the middle child. But in the end, things hadn't worked out, so they went their separate ways, as so often happens these days. He was the only real duck hunter I knew as a youth and was the one who got me started in the sport of waterfowling. Obviously, Jack wasn't wasting any time hunting that morning so he must have been out riding around when he spotted my vehicle parked alongside the road and decided to stop to see how we were doing.

As the geese closed the distance at a steady pace, Darren and I decided to do the only proactive thing we could, blow on our duck calls! After all, it wasn't going to hurt to try and sound like a couple of contented hen mallards sitting on a pond, even though the blocks looked just like the inanimate objects they were. We started out tentatively but as the geese kept coming our brashness grew, giving us the audacity to call even louder. There we were, trying to squeeze ourselves into the mud, geese bearing down on us, with an audience watching the entire event unfold. When the small flock broke over the last vestige of woods, it was obvious that they were losing altitude. This was unbelievable, there was absolutely no reason why these birds should be duped by our set up, or our calling, but they were. Over the far west end of the pond, they were in full "set down mode," honking all the way in. I whispered to Darren several times, "Wait until the first few are in the water, wait, wait, wait." The duck calls dropped away from our mouths to our chests almost simultaneously and the guns were readied for the impending action.

It looked as though the birds were going to fly over the hole and sit down at the east end of the decoys. Again, I urged Darren to hold his fire until the first few geese set down before taking those still in the air. That way I figured all of them would be in range for both of us and, if necessary, we could have shots at birds coming off the water. No more did the words come out of my mouth when Darren jumped up. Having no choice, I sprang up too, bringing the gun to my shoulder. As we rose out of the quagmire, the birds hit the brakes and started flailing to get out of there. Six shots rang out about as fast as two hunters can fire six shots. I know that my first shot was directed at nothing in particular. Realizing it though, I took great care to pick out a bird for the second and third shots. I'd like to tell you that we had geese falling from the sky in quantity but that would be a lie. Initially I was sure I scored on my second shot. The goose appeared to be hit, but as often happens birds can go through all sorts of contortions to get away, some of which look very unnatural, as if they have been struck, when in actuality they were never touched. Darren and I watched as the flock gathered up and headed back in the direction from which they came, all of them flying strongly. We ended up with nothing.

Everything had come together perfectly — even though it shouldn't have. They were right in our laps and we blew it — big time! I don't know if we had waited a few seconds longer if things would have worked out any better, but I turned to Darren and scolded him for getting up too soon. He didn't argue the point and we both felt badly enough not to discuss it any further. We also knew that we were going to get quite a razing from his old man who had stuck around to witness the whole damn thing. Taking a goose or two that still, autumn morning would have been the sweetest of success, but the show was over and neither of us felt like sitting there any longer. Darren and I talked little as we gathered up our decoys and walked towards the truck. I think Jack realized that we were in no mood to relive our folly because he drove off before we even reached the road. While it's not always the case, time does heal most wounds and we were already making plans for our next hunt as I pulled into the yard to drop Darren off. As he exited the truck, I told him, "Say hello to your old man and tell him we ended up with nothing, you know, a big, fat goose egg!"

Chapter 6

Tar Sand, Muskeg and Bears

I glanced at my watch: Thirty-five minutes and my first bear hunt would end and a week of midnight suppers, trips through the muskeg and unforgettable memories would be history. Just as my mind was recounting the week's events, a noise caught my attention. Again, I heard it, behind me and to my right. Turning my head ever so slowly toward the source, I caught a glimpse of a black ghost drifting toward me through the woods at a cautious, measured pace. Usually at this point, my pulse would quicken, my breathing would become labored and my mind would race to keep the rest of me together. It didn't happen, and instead, I was relaxed, almost placid. The bear ambled along, stopping momentarily to drink from a small stream tumbling toward the lake behind me. I was safely strapped to a tree and in a stand some fifteen feet in the air. A well-used bait station was a mere sixteen yards away. The bear kept coming, furtively exploring its surroundings with nose, ears and eyes. As the bear got closer I started my assessment, coal black coat, no rub marks, average sized adult. Certainly not the big brute I was hoping for. Finally the bruin was there, nosing the bait site, making sure it was safe to approach. It had gone three quarters of a circle around me by now and was angling from my left to right. I conducted another self-diagnosis, still calm, cool and collected. My bow hand settled into the grip of my recurve, the fingers of my left hand found their position on the string; the decision had been made.

These were the final minutes of my inaugural Canadian bear hunt — a week when I learned a lot about the bush of northeastern Alberta, bears, and bear hunting. Darren was, once again, my companion during our stay in Canada. Like me, he wasn't sure what to expect from this adventure. We had viewed the prerequisite videos, read back issues of bowhunting magazines and practiced on our 3-D McKenzie bear targets and we still felt a little trepidation on our journey to the north woods. Arriving in Ft. McMurray, we were toting a Robertson recurve and longbow respectively, questionable tackle, in some people's minds, given the nature of our quarry! The trip hadn't been thought about or planned much in advance. We had actually been talking about doing an elk hunt for our next out-of-state expedition but as fate would have it, we found ourselves in the northern Boreal forest the last week of May. Ft. McMurray was a lot bigger than I had expected. This northern outpost is built around the world's only commercial production of synthetic oil from tar sands. Tar sand, as I came to learn, is a deposit of loose sand that is saturated with bitumen, a degraded remnant of oil. The largest known deposits of tar sands are found around Ft. McMurray in the Athabasca River valley.

Our first evening hunt introduced us to a rolling landscape heavily wooded and dissected by sphagnum moss bogs fondly referred to as muskeg or "the keg." The land would be inaccessible except for the cut-lines crisscrossing the area that are a result of tar sand exploration. Not only would it be difficult to navigate through this country but it would also be next to impossible to hunt bear there, other than over bait. As would be the case for the remainder of the week, Darren went one way and I another. That first evening found me in a treestand, which I felt was a little too close to the ground given the fact that we were hunting bear. Chris McKinnon, our guide for the week, told me a good-sized black was visiting the site and had been seen two days earlier. Just a couple of hours into my first bear hunt I heard heavy, shuffling foot steps behind me. I didn't dare look, or move for that matter. This bear caught me comfortably seated on my behind, a situation I try to avoid. He ended up eight yards to my right, the one place where I didn't have a shot. The bear was at ease, foraging on early spring shoots. After several minutes, it finally decided to check out a beaver hung from a suspended pole at the bait site directly in front of me. It comically stood upright reaching for the decaying carcass, nearly falling over backward as it strained to reach the tasty morsel. As it came down on all fours, I was positioning myself to come to full draw. Waiting for the bear to move into a good position for the shot, I realized that the wind had shifted and was directly at my back, a fact that the bear verified at almost the same instant. Bears don't start off as quick as a whitetail, but once motivated they move surprisingly fast. I looked on in amazement as the bear ran dead away, down the hill into the muskeg. My day afield ended as I watched the sun dip ever so slowly below the tree line. Back at camp, we gathered in the cook tent for an early morning supper. I'm not sure I ever ate such a big meal so late, or should I say, so early in the day.

After a very short night, we took it easy the next morning, shooting our bows and discussing what we were looking for in a bear. Big blacks versus medium sized cinnamons versus blondes of any size. Mid-afternoon found us headed out for another long sit. I went to the same stand I hunted the first evening, although we repositioned it to account for the wind direction and the bear's previous approach. Darren, on the other hand, headed for a new stand. As he and Chris approached, they caught a fleeting glimpse of a bear in close proximity to the bait. They snuck in but the bear was nowhere to be seen. Later, with nightfall approaching, a shadowy figure moved toward Darren's stand, but just as it got within bow range, it spooked. Within a few minutes, the bear stalked the bait a second time. Again, only a few steps away from Darren's shooting lane, it tentatively moved off. Just before dark the bear attempted, one last time, to slink its way into the bait. Darren, patient as he could be, sat tight looking for an opportunity to release an arrow. This time the bruin kept coming and Darren got his shot. The third time was a charm. When he and Chris came to pick me up, Darren succinctly related his story to me, "We've got a bear to pack out in the morning!" All I saw that evening was a ruffed grouse budding in the aspen trees surrounding my stand. During our midnight supper, Chris told us that we'd be going through "the keg" for the next day's hunt. I wasn't exactly sure what to expect, but just the way he said it left me feeling a little anxious.

We got up relatively early the next morning in order to retrieve Darren's trophy. Chris, Darren and I walked from the tree, where Darren sat the night before, in the direction where he last saw the bear as it hightailed out of there. We hadn't gone far when we found it on the hillside among the aspen and spruce, all of sixty yards from where it stood when Darren released his arrow. He had made a great shot. That afternoon we headed into some new country via all-terrain vehicles (ATVs). With a two bear limit in Alberta, Darren was able to continue hunting. It was on this trip that I appreciated how far we had been, and would continue to be, hunting from one another. The average distance between our stands on any given evening was approximately ten miles. To get to our new haunt we had to cross a serious stretch of muskeg. It didn't appear to be all that far across initially, but after our first time through, "the keg" seemed like it was five miles long, rather than the half a mile it actually was. Muskeg could be defined as sphagnum moss, mud and water whipped into a cocktail of mush, not unlike soupy oatmeal. ATVs can go through a lot but if you ever want to seriously test drive one find some muskeg. We actually walked, pushed, pulled and waded more than we rode. Thank God for knee high rubber boots, great rain gear and duct tape. That combination of essential paraphernalia kept me dry on our many ventures through "the keg."

Over the course of the next three days, Darren and I saw numerous bears but he was into them thicker than I was except for a sow and three yearlings I had the pleasure to thoroughly observe and enjoy. She and her cubs habituated a bait site I hunted one evening. They were there when I went in and treed a hundred yards behind my stand. The sow was a nervous sort; paranoid schizophrenic would probably be a more apt description. For two hours they stayed in those trees, then, one by one, they descended. After they were all on the ground, they started to head in my direction. The troop would advance several yards when, without obvious cause, the sow would "woof" the cubs up into the trees. They'd come down, progress a few more yards and she'd do it again. This went on for more than half an hour. Those cubs sure got a work out that night! Two of the yearlings ended up directly under my treestand. They found my rain gear and bow case draped neatly in the underbrush drying out from our journey through the muskeg. I thought they'd carry it all off for sure as they played with them like puppies play with a grouse wing. Fortunately, they lost interest and left it all intact. I was also certain that the sow, which was thirty yards behind me, would put them up into the trees again. This time they'd have to come up mine and I wasn't real big on that. However, the four of them continued on their way and I was happy just to have had the opportunity to experience it all.

After several more adventures through the muskeg, short nights, early morning suppers, and close calls, it was decided that I would spend my last twilight hours in the north woods adjacent to Sucker Lake. I was to have hunted this bait three days earlier but when we got there, a pair of biologists was camped a hundred yards down the shoreline conducting a fish survey on the lake so we trucked off to another bait site some five miles away. That was the same evening I had the experience with the sow and three yearlings. The biologists were flown out the next day when Darren sat the bait and had seen several bears. Earlier that last evening, I also had two small bears, one black and the other blonde, visit the bait. But now I was there in the waning minutes of my hunt with a beautiful bear broadside at sixteen yards. At that moment, everything came together, so much so that it was almost surreal, as though I was under the direction, the control of a greater force. Bringing the bow to full draw, I became transfixed on a spot low, and a third of the way back, on the bear's flank. I was as cool as a cucumber. This isn't normal for me; usually I'm fighting to concentrate on a spot and trying not to rush the shot. This was different though, in a very good way and before I knew it the arrow had disappeared behind my quarry's shoulder. The bruin wheeled and sped away straight up the hill. Then it happened, a crash, several wailing moans, and then silence. It was over. The end of that bear's life is an experience I will never forget. I had heard about the "death moan" numerous times, but until you hear it, you can't begin to know how it sounds and even more how it makes you feel. Chris must have had a premonition because he told me he would come in to pick me up a little early but would hang back a mile or so and wait until dark before approaching the stand site. He told me to come and get him if I had any luck so we could get the bear and start back to camp in the fading daylight. I did just that. Fifteen minutes after the shot, we were headed up the hill to find my bear. It went eighty yards and expired from a perfectly placed arrow. The Athabascan bear was beautiful, its coat was thick and ebony black and not a hair was out of place. What a wonderful animal, one perfectly suited for the environment it called home.

We rode out through the muskeg one last time under the light of a nearly full moon. It was one trip that I didn't mind taking at all knowing that a trophy of a lifetime accompanied me back to camp; a trophy that was hard earned, and taken quickly and cleanly with two sticks and a string. A trophy that, like me, lived the best way it knew how from one day to the next and a trophy that will be forever immortalized in my heart and soul.

CHAPTER 7

Timberdoodle Memories

It was Easter Sunday a few years back and my family and I had gathered at my sister's place for dinner and birthday celebrations. The anniversary of my birth occasionally falls on Easter, and Darren, my ever-present hunting partner and kindred spirit, was born the day before my sixth birthday. Easter has been, ever since I can remember, a time not only to praise our Lord and Savior and contemplate what He means to us, but also an opportunity to celebrate yet another year under our belts. My sister had recently moved into the clan's old homestead, located just ten miles south of Lake Ontario. Growing up there was, for me, akin to most kids growing up in a rural setting during the midst of the baby boom generation. To get groceries, buy clothes or go out to eat meant taking the car and driving into town some five miles away. All through my school days, I was the first one on the bus in the morning and last one off at night and the ride was the better part of an hour. We had farmers for neighbors and cattle inhabited pastures directly to the east and west of our little place. Our modest chunk of Mother Earth consisted of open fields, an old orchard, a brush lot and a first order stream that could bloom into a small lake given the right conditions. The family farm was flat, somewhat poorly drained and had a history as a small cheese factory back in the good old days. Growing up there was relatively easy and mostly fun.

We had stuffed ourselves with ham and all the fixings and partook in the obligatory cake and ice cream when I decided to step out onto the back porch and enjoy the twilight sky painted in azure and burnt orange as the sun escaped to start a new day in some faraway land. My kids were little at the time and they joined me as I stooped on the rail quietly contemplating my childhood home, growing up, and family and friends who are no longer with us. As we stood there enjoying one of life's precious moments I heard a familiar sound emanating from what was once a crop field but had since grown up into brush and forbs barely hinting of its once productive past as far as corn, oats and hay are concerned. The noise was a familiar one to me, although I would guess it would be a mystery to most people. I drew the kids' attention to it by pointing in the general direction of its origin each time I heard it. Whispering, "Hear it? There! Listen." Melissa and Justin whispered back, "Dad, what is that?" "Wait," I said. "listen, there's more!" Then it stopped. After a short interlude, we heard the sound of whistling wings, as the source of the sonant ascended heavenward, spiraling to a height where it just about disappeared into the dimly lit firmament. Act three began as the creature sideslipped earth bound, like a falling leaf, chirping all the way to the ground. Then the sound, that "peent," started up again. What a spectacle to be able to witness, especially with impressionable children at your side, and how brilliant one feels when you can actually explain what's happening and why. Repeatedly the little bird put on its display, not for us of course, but for an opportunity to contribute to its specie's gene pool. We were just the benefactors of the male American woodcock's early spring courting ritual. The cover he had chosen to use as his courtyard was perfect in every way, with a good mix of saplings and shrubs, having a high stem count, yet with extensive patches of nearly barren ground suitable for both nesting cover and the probing of delectable earthworms. Um, um good!

Woodcock are strange little birds for sure. The fact that they are camouflaged in a dead leaf pattern (perfect for their environs), migratory and eat worms is relatively normal in the avian community. But given that they have long probing bills, sometimes fly like helicopters with navigational problems, rarely escape more than a hundred yards when hunted, and have such an elaborate mating ritual makes them a wee bit different. I also don't personally know anyone who claims to be a woodcock hunter. There are duck hunters, pheasant hunters and grouse hunters but there is no one, that I am aware of, that is a self-proclaimed woodcock aficionado. Therefore, the quirky, diminutive bird gets very little attention and what they do get is usually shared with others, such as the more noble ruffed grouse.

All this leads me to the memory I have of hunting these ignoble little birds in western New York more than a decade ago. The hunt started out like so many others had. After donning my brush pants and wool jacket, I grabbed my Remington 870, gathered up the dogs and hoofed it to the woods behind my house. Being able to hunt in your own "backyard" is an extremely valuable commodity and I have been fortunate for the past quarter century to be able to take advantage of just that no matter where I have lived. My English springer spaniel, Abby, and German shorthaired pointer, Tracie, who worked extremely well together, accompanied me. Tracie had the better nose and ranged a bit further than Abby. Abby on the other hand covered ground thoroughly and never lost a downed bird. Tracie always hunted with flushing dogs and was never "trained" to point, which suited me just fine — I was brought up with birds flushing wildly from the cover, some within range, others not — that was just the way we hunted. This combination of canine assistants worked very well for grouse and pheasants, which, for the most part, were never found more than a brace at a time. As we hit the cover late that afternoon, my intentions were to add a grouse or two to the freezer. I knew the area well and thought the goal to be attainable. Conditions were conducive for an early autumn hunt. A significant number of leaves had hit the ground but many were still clinging to the trees awaiting colder and windier conditions. It was cool and dank, perfect for a hunter and two dogs to slink through the woods. We hit several good coverts with a flush or two but no decent shooting opportunities presented themselves.

It was early yet and I decided to veer off my intended route and check out some new country. These impromptu side trips were often dual purposed. Not only was I looking for good bird cover, I was also constantly scouting for deer sign on my forays through the woods in order to enhance my chances while bowhunting. Looking back on it now I realize that my ardent pursuit of game birds was waning and bowhunting was becoming more and more a part of my life. But at that time, I was still trying to do it all, as youth and few commitments in life will allow one to do. The dogs and I crossed a narrow ravine and marched uphill to a small plateau, maybe four or five acres in size. The area looked to be an old field and was covered with clumps of aspen and alders interspersed with goldenrod and other herbaceous vegetation. As I worked around the undulating edges, the dogs took to the cover. It wasn't long before I heard the distinctive twittering whistle of a woodcock taking flight from an aspen grove. I only caught a glimpse of him as he zig-zagged his way through the trees. When I started to follow up, another bird took off behind me. Two birds up and no shots taken! Deciding to step back into the clearing, I let the dogs do their thing. Walking quickly between thin spots in the cover, I paused in each of them in order to create clear shooting lanes to be able to venture a shot or two if given the opportunity. As I eased along, another bird took flight, then another. I had found woodcock heaven. Ruminating on it a bit, I conjured up the notion that I must have happened into a flock of flight birds working their way through the area. They had stopped in a perfect spot to rest and fuel up before venturing further south. Realizing we needed to take our time hunting the relatively small patch of real estate, the dogs and I started to comb the area more methodically when I finally got a good clean shot at one of those little devils as it attempted to go from one clump of aspen to another, and dropped him in mid-flight. Abby diligently picked him up and brought him to hand. Examining it closely, I brushed back the variegated feathers of the little cock bird, concentrating on his long bill and bulging dark eyes. Strange little birds indeed!

The dogs and I had just completed a circuit around the old field when another timberdoodle took flight rising straight up through the poplars emblazoned in fall's yellow hews absent their summer time chlorophyll. I brought my gun up and quickly fired a round in the bird's general direction. Too low! As the woodcock leveled off,

I yanked the trigger again and dropped him very near the spot from which he originated. It's hard to tell how many birds were in the "flock" but I'd venture a guess that there were at least a dozen. We took two and moved the rest around quit a bit. That was enough fun for one day so the dogs and I headed home as the sun sought refuge behind the hills to the west.

As I completed the chore of dressing the birds, it occurred to me that it would be nice to go back and try to harvest a woodcock to add to my slowly growing taxidermy collection. That's all I needed to rationalize a return trip to my newly discovered honey hole the following day. Upon my arrival home after work I went through the same routine I'd gone through the day before. Making sure I had an ample supply of shotshells in my pocket, I got the dogs and away we went. Instead of hitting my grouse haunts, we went directly to the old field. The weather hadn't changed, the dogs were in good spirits and I was all hopped-up ready for action. Other than being a little earlier than we were the previous day, everything was identical. As we worked the cover, the dogs would get birdy but nothing would show itself. We ventured into, and out of, every clump of trees we encountered. The dogs would "get hot" over and over again but to no avail. We completed our round trip of the field without a single flush. I decided that we'd try it again, going deeper into the cover, ghosting our initial route. Again nothing! Whether it was the fact that we had stirred things up the day before or it was just time for the birds to fly south, I don't know but there was no question that they were gone. Even the dogs looked perplexed and frustrated. They could pick up scent here and there but couldn't find anything at the end of the trail. Other than finding a few probe holes in the soft, friable soil and droppings scattered all about, we left the old field with only memories of an exciting encounter with a fall flight of timberdoodles. The spot I had picked out on the mantle would have to remain vacant: There was deer sign to find and grouse to chase!

CHAPTER 8

From My Perch in the Woods

I strained my eyes to read the watch face in the predawn darkness
of a late October day to find out it was 6:40 a.m. It had taken me
more than twenty minutes to skulk the half mile into my stand
located in the mixed hardwoods behind my home. My jaunt in was
a good one. The soggy leaves on the forest floor and steady southwest zephyr made it easy for my clodhopper-supported frame to
glide along almost noiselessly. In addition, I wasn't cognizant of
stirring any of the wood's inhabitants to the point that would neg-
atively affect my hunt.

I settled in to become one with the murky grove, nocked a
cedar shaft and tuned my senses to that which enveloped me. As
Aurora ushered in the day's first rays of light in the eastern sky, a
barred owl lit on a small tree a mere fifteen yards away. Not satisfied with his perch, he effortlessly winged to a higher venue to gain
a better perspective. He now sat motionless thirty feet away listening, watching and waiting for one more morsel before ending his

nightlong pursuit of sustenance. He and I were there for the same thing and hunting in the same manner. However, there was one difference: He needed to kill to be successful and I didn't.

The sun had officially risen but remained sequestered behind a ridge from which emanated the faint sounds of turkey talk. It sounded like a small flock had recently hit the ground and was drifting in my general direction. Their day and mine was just starting. Turning to spy on my friend the owl, all I saw was the faint glow of gold and amber leaves where he once was perched. He had probably retired to a roost in the tall and sodden hemlocks down in the creek bottom, which drains the wildlife-laden watershed where I had taken a stand.

The day awakened fully, as the movements and sounds of an increasing number of woodland denizens became more evident in the intensifying radiance. I eased my head around to the west to catch the end flight of a ruffed grouse as it jettisoned itself into an ancient apple tree just twenty yards away. It looked as though his breakfast would, at least in part, consist of sun-ripened fruit. As the day matured, I heard the whir of wings and whistling communiqués of wood ducks flying overhead. I endeavored to pick out their low, frenetic flight but was unable to do so through the tenacious autumn leaves. Rays of sun filtered their way through the sylvan scene striking the sides of trees soaked from the heavy rain that fell the prior evening. Steam rose up and swirled in the breeze, which was still fixed in my favor, as I awaited the hoof-falls of my intended quarry.

Time steadily marched on, as it always does, waiting for no one, never missing a beat, nor caring about the activity or lack thereof, which occurs within its frame. But I was investing these precious moments in doing something I love, something that makes me feel whole and in sync with the natural rhythms of our terrestrial sphere. The distant honking of geese caught my attention. Geese often times sound different to me.

On some occasions, their cackling sounds playful, almost child-like. At other times, their melodious tones seem mournful. This day, however, their song speaks of purpose. The talk is of finding food and getting serious about their southward flight. Again, I glanced upward to locate their approaching v-shaped signature in the sky pointed toward a more equatorial clime. I'm not sure what it is, but I cannot hear geese and ignore them. Something deep inside compels me to find them and confirm their numbers, formation and direction of flight. I finally spied their long-necked forms through the intricate network of leaves, twigs and branches that did their best to obscure my view. One, two, three…thirteen in all. Was this a sign?

As the goose talk faded in the distance, I became aware of the effects of rising out of bed in the early morning solitude and standing stock-still for several hours. The muscles in my back and shoulders started to ache, which I attribute more to poor posture than to my advancing age. I decided it was time to succumb to the familiar seat of my treestand. It would provide me with a little relief as it gave me an opportunity to change my position and rest my weary back. I have found that the majority of stands are not built for people of my size and shape. Six feet four inches isn't exceptionally tall, but I have long legs and the seats of treestands are generally way too low for my satisfaction. But on this day, it would provide a modicum of succor and allow me to stay in the woods a little longer. After surveying my environs thoroughly I slowly eased down into the seat and rocked myself into a comfortable position. No sooner did I settle in than I caught a familiar movement out in front of me. Deer!

Was it a buck, doe or fawn? I couldn't tell. Slowly easing a grunt tube to my mouth I let out a few subtle grunts. The whitetail moved parallel to my position and disappeared. I kept searching the brush for something familiar, an ear or a leg, anything that would confirm the deer's presence. Finally, a figure began to emerge from a tangle of saplings, grapevines and briars. Then another and another: a doe with two fawns! As they worked their way through the woods, the doe and one of the fawns started to angle toward me. They were in no hurry. It still amazes me how long a deer may stand in one spot while inspecting its surroundings. Apparently, their sense of time, if they have any at all, is far different from ours! They took several steps, stopped, grazed on a few forbs and browsed on a twig or two. Eventually they ended up thirty yards out in front of me, totally oblivious of my presence.

I slowly pulled a second grunt tube from my jacket. It imitates not only buck grunts, but also produces doe and fawn bleats. I had lost track of the second sibling and wondered if the doe shared in my curiosity as to its whereabouts. Doing my best to sound like a lost, forlorn fawn the doe snapped to attention with eyes, ears and nose searching for her "progeny." She turned toward me and started to ease closer to my hide. The doe continued her investigation, but couldn't confirm with her other senses what she had heard with her antenna-like ears. The remaining fawn trailed close behind attempting to emulate the doe, exploring the underbrush for its likeness. They continued their advance. At fifteen yards, the doe offered me several shot opportunities, but at that time and place I was not interested in harvesting what would be, under other circumstances, a fine trophy. After all, I had done everything right. I chose the right stand, on the right wind. I snuck in undetected. I hunted with patience and, at least in my mind, called the deer into my effective bow range.

After closely scrutinizing my hideout, the doe and fawn started to amble away still looking back occasionally for the nonexistent fawn. They ultimately hooked up with the third member of the party and headed off. As they eased along through the woods, the hoarse yelping of a turkey became my focal point. I intently watched for the birds hoping they'd come my way. Turkey season was open and I had two tags in my fanny pack. Suddenly, several dark silhouettes appeared below me at a distance. A small flock of jakes scratched their way along the leaf littered forest floor. They momentarily mingled with the doe and fawns then proceeded toward a mast laden beech tree ridge. The sun's rays would warm them nicely as they whiled away the remainder of the day. They completely avoided me as I spied on them from my perch — oh well!

Time had advanced on to the predetermined hour when I needed to leave and head off to one of life's never ending commitments. I saw no bucks. The quarry, which I intended to harvest, failed to show itself. I never released an arrow. And I didn't even pull my recurve back, other than the obligatory warm-up upon my arrival in the stand! Was my day successful? You bet it was. Bowhunting to me is far more than a method of harvesting game: It's a spiritual experience where I can observe nature and become one with it. I can participate as a full and equal member in the circle of life, not just view it as an outsider or use it as a resource. I took no trophy home that day. I hope the owl fared better than I did. He needed to, I didn't.

CHAPTER 9

Look What I Found

The old saying goes something like "Good luck finds you when opportunity meets preparation" and I honestly subscribe to that line of thinking. But I am also enough of a realist to know that sometimes you just step in it and come out smelling like a bouquet of spring flowers. This doesn't happen to me often, but it has happened and strangely enough, it's occurred several times while in pursuit of ducks. Now I don't want to give the impression that I'm a die-hard duck hunter. I know several serious duck hunters and I cannot include myself among them. However, I have hunted ducks since the time I was old enough to carry a scatter gun into the marsh. And I have hunted them in almost every conceivable manner, from hunting divers, coursing their way along the Great Lakes, over a huge spread of decoys to jump shooting puddlers while slogging through swamps with nothing more than my gun, a pocket full of shells and, every now and then, a pair of waders that didn't leak.

While ferreting out my webbed footed friends, I have hunted a variety of waterlogged landforms, some good, some not so good. Many of which I have had the opportunity to explore and scout, some however; I have not. Quite a few years ago, more than I like to think about actually, I heard about some good waterfowling to be had on a stretch of state-owned property along the St. Lawrence River, some four hours drive time north of my home. In fact, it was so good that one had to apply for a permit through a lottery to be able to hunt the opening weekend of the season. I shared this news with my brother Bob and his son RJ and the three of us applied, as a party, for a permit. Lo and behold we were drawn our first time in and had the privilege to hunt the area come the season opener. Unfortunately, none of us had ever been near the place, so we were going in blind. Not hunting out a blind mind you, we just had no idea what the landscape even looked like. And due to our work schedules, compounded by the distance up there, none of us were able to get a chance to scope things out.

We arrived very early opening day, after driving half the night, to find scores of our duck hunting brethren parked along an access road waiting for the gate to be open. This was new to all of us and we felt terribly uneasy with the situation. After getting out of the truck in the murky blackness of the wee hours of the morning and stretching a bit, we made some inquires as to the lay of the land and suggestions as to where we might go. As you might expect, we got a lot of very general information and no enlightenment as to where any particularly good hunting could be had. Most of our comrades had small johnboats or canoes, large racks of decoys and an over exuberant Lab. Conversely, we had waders, a bag of decoys and travel weary bodies. We sat and waited, for what seemed to be an inordinate amount of time, for a uniformed employee of the state to come along and unlock the gate. All hell broke loose as the barrier swung open and people raced to their vehicles, tearing off down the gravel thoroughfare that ran through the place to get to their hunting Mecca. We had no clue as to where to go. All we knew was that there was "big water" out there someplace, along with channels and smaller ponds randomly distributed throughout the vicinity. We drove down the road a ways and came upon a pull off that didn't look like the parking lot of a McDonald's at midday. Throwing our gear on our backs, we noticed a trail along a ditch that we had been told led to open water. Off we went, flashlights clenched in our teeth, looking nearly as foolish as we felt. I don't know about you, but I just loathe that sick feeling that you get in the pit of your stomach when you know that you are absolutely clueless about a given situation. And right about then an extreme case of nausea was overtaking me.

Our "trail" soon disintegrated into nothing. We still had the ditch to guide us though, so on we went, crashing through the alder and willow brush like a rut-crazed bull moose. There we were, going someplace, we didn't know where, and the burgeoning light of the eastern sky was indicating that we better get there before it was too late. The feeling in my gut was getting worse. We had driven nearly two hundred miles, waited what seemed like hours for a gate attendant and now were going to miss the most precious minutes of the day trying to find out where the hell we were.

We forged on and suddenly an oasis began to materialize — I could see where the thicket was beginning to thin and glimpsed what looked like open water up ahead. After struggling through the last remnants of the brush, we broke out into an opening probably ten acres or so in size. The area was dominated by cattails and was betwixt the junk we had just come through and an island of hardwoods that separated the morass from the open water. As I said before, I don't consider myself a serious duck hunter but I do know good wetland habitat when I see it and I was standing smack dab in the middle of it. Not only that, but as far as I could tell we were the only ones there. Due to the increasing daylight, and the sound of whistling wings overhead, there was no time for a discussion, let alone consensus building about whether to stay or move on so I said, "This is it, load up your guns and let's do a little duck hunting!"

We didn't even parcel out the dozen or so decoys we had with us. The three of us just spread out a bit and hid away among the tall reeds adjacent to a fairly large pothole and waited for legal shooting time to arrive. A short time later, the tranquility of early

morn was shattered by what sounded like artillery fire on the big water out in front of us. A huge flock of geese had gotten up and the boys were letting go with everything they had. Looking back at it, I think a lot of the folks that we had spoken with earlier were there for the express purpose of getting into those geese, which was all fine and good, but we were there for what would hopefully be a steadier flight of ducks. Shortly after the battery range opened, we started eyeballing ducks flying in from all directions, sizing-up the area. They appeared as singles, doubles and small flocks. Wood ducks, blacks, mallards, widgeon, blue-wing and green-wing teal started searching for a safe haven where they could set down and loaf away the remainder of the day. And there we were, sitting in the catbird seat, by sheer happenstance, whispering back and forth about how many we could see and where they were coming from. For the next hour, we enjoyed some pretty fast and furious shooting, as birds couldn't resist the temptation of our little honey hole. The smell of combusted gunpowder filled the stagnant, moisture-laden air around us — we were in heaven. After things slowed down a bit, we took care to start picking up spent shotshells and total the morning's take. I have never been one to feel compelled to take a daily limit to call a hunt a success from the harvest standpoint, but the forenoon's shooting had been so good we were only two birds shy, and along with the fact that we had come so far we felt the need, and the desire, to obtain our quota if we could.

The sun now shone down on us from its position above the trees and although there were birds in the air, they were flying high and hard searching for digs that were more hospitable. I decided to head out and do a little swamp busting hoping to jump shoot a duck or two in order to call it a day. I had trudged a couple hundred yards and was sweating bullets as I fought my way through the mud and the muck, when I caught a movement out of the corner of my eye. An immature greenhead was setting his wings looking to take refuge in a nearby mud hole. Hunkering down, I kept my face hidden so as not to have the duck flare off. Fortunately for me, no one in the surrounding environs took a shot, an event that would most certainly cause the bird to gain altitude in a hurry. He kept coming like a fighter jet looking to land on a carrier deck. With the bird's landing gear down and locked, and wings furiously beating to lower himself into the pool of water just yards away, I jumped up and made a quick, albeit accurate shot. The young bird splashed down where he had intended to land. While retrieving my prize, a shot rang out from behind me. One lone, very decisive sounding shot. Immediately, I knew that either Bob or RJ had ended the day's hunt.

We had obviously happened on to a very nice spot and evidently, one that no one else either knew about or cared about. We hunted that same slough for several years until I moved even further away and daily limits were drastically reduced due to dwindling duck populations. Fortunately, we always experienced excellent shooting and never had any competition from other hunters.

Several years later, having relocated to western New York, I once again found myself seeking out new duck hunting haunts. And again, as I had in the past, I looked to public land to fill the bill. This time the setting was a large expanse of wooded swamps and marshland on the lake plain juxtaposed to lakes Erie and Ontario. Given my previous experience on state-owned property I took some time and made an effort to scout the area thoroughly. In addition to obtaining a few maps and aerial photos, I drove around the site looking for likely spots to intercept and lure in ducks. In short, I was prepared, or so I thought!

Opening morning found me hunting on my own, but again I had plenty of company, as the roadways throughout the property were dotted with vehicles of all makes and models. While I prepared to go afield, several parties started off down a dike, the same one I intended to use as access to what I felt would be a good location to set up. I'm not anti-social by nature but when I'm hunting, I prefer to be alone or at the very most hunt only with members of my own party. As I witnessed yet another group of hunters head out in the direction I had planned to go myself, my intentions instantly changed. I did a one-eighty and took off for parts totally unknown. So there I was again, opening day of duck season and seemingly no place to go.

Looking for a spot conducive to carrying out the day's objective, I maneuvered my way along a field edge in the pitch black. Either I have a nose for this type of thing or else I'm just darn lucky in the truest sense of the word, because as I went along I noticed a bit of water at the field's edge. Easing through a hedgerow to investigate, I found myself looking at a beautiful wooded swamp overflowing with duckweed-laden water. Pausing to survey my new environs, a duck exploded from the surface just a few yards away. It was still pretty gloomy but I could tell that this place looked good. I advanced only a few steps and waited until the light of day helped me to assess the situation. With dawn fast approaching, I realized the swamp was chock full of downed trees and stumps. You couldn't take two steps without having to climb over something. Thank God for long legs! This time it was immediately evident to me why there wasn't another soul in sight: This was a hellhole! As if on cue, birds started to work the skies around me, and it soon became apparent that there were also a number of birds sitting tight in the seemingly impenetrable swamp. I slowly and carefully worked my way along, not wanting to take an unscheduled bath, and quickly decided to take up a position where I could pass shoot birds winging their way to breakfast. My shooting of the day's first bird, a woody, marked legal shooting time. Clawing my way through the tangled mass to retrieve the bird, another pair of nature's more spectacular specimens buzzed over me and I pulled up quickly and cleanly missed as they screamed across the deck away from me. With a bird in hand, I took up my vigil waiting for more action. A blue-winged teal skittered into gun range, and not hesitating a bit I locked on and dumped him with a single load of steel shot.

The birds seemed to be coming out of nowhere, with little or no warning, as the timber that stood ominously around me cast its tenebrous shadows inhibiting the illumination of my venue with the aging of the day. Given those conditions, and certainly not an indication of my shooting ability, I missed a few more birds than usual that morning. Even so, I was having a great time. A pair of mallards eventually dumped into the opposite end of the swamp and for some unknown reason I decided to go after them. To say this place was a jungle would be an understatement, but I actually feel that the birds felt safe there, knowing that anything my size wouldn't close the distance quickly. After what seemed like an eternity, I had cautiously approached to within good gun range as the birds started to get antsy. Now each arduous stride was carefully measured in order for me to be able to take a steady shot upon their rise. Off they went and I miraculously ended the morning with a perfect double, two birds with two shots!

Unfortunately, the existence of this small piece of duck nirvana was short lived. Whether it was only meant to be temporary or someone's objectives changed, I went back to find the area completely devoid of water as a result of management practices by the state wildlife agency. As it came to pass, it didn't matter much anyway because I once again moved away from the area, headed off to new hunting grounds many miles away.

Fast forward a few years, to find a man who had let duck hunting slip down the list of outdoor pursuits and his son, Justin, coming of age as far as the shooting sports are concerned. Knowing full well that Justin was interested in hunting anything and everything, and wanting to give him the opportunity to do just that, I found myself checking over the gear I had and buying what I needed in order to expose my boy to the grand sport of waterfowling. After a few productive ventures afield, Justin and I prepared for our local opening day. We had two good possibilities lined up. We could hunt a nearby river that we had previously scouted or a lake we frequented with our canoe fishing for bass, perch and pickerel, which I felt might provide for some inviting duck hangouts. Given the tight cover of the sinuous river we decided to hunt the more open waters of the lake. I had three or four spots, around the lake's shallow, north end, tucked away in my mind that I presumed would make likely ambush sites.

Justin and I got an early start that first morning hoping to beat the locals to the best spots. When we arrived at the access point on the lake, there was no one around and in workmanlike fashion, we unloaded the canoe and gear from the truck and prepared to set out. We would head off for, what I surmised would be, the most promising location on the water to stake a claim, a natural funnel where the main feeder creek entered the impoundment. Just before we embarked, three pickups came rolling in, each filled with anxious hunters. Talking with each party and inquiring where they intended to go, I heard every piece of my game plan described to a tee. Unbelievable! I had no idea that this unlikely lake in the middle of nowhere would attract so much attention. I fired back at the gang to ascertain if anyone would be hunting out in one of the lake's small backwater bays. They replied with a not so reassuring, "Not that we know of." Turning to Justin I said, "Let's go — we may not see a duck but we'll give it a try anyway." I continued to lower expectations from the moment our paddles began to slice through the water to the point when we stood in a swatch of cattails overlooking our small decoy spread in the dun of early dawn. Even though the area looked promising, it was small and ringed by huge hemlocks that limited access to our winged quarry. I was sure we'd see something but I didn't know what or how many.

The shooting started early on the big water as Justin and I waited for ducks and increasing light to brighten our dark, little hole. Suddenly a small flock of woodies flew directly at us from a beaver flow located on the upper reaches of the creek. And with a bit of poetic justice they skirted right behind the party that occupied our day's primary destination. Justin fired first and I backed him up, although he didn't require it as we each downed a bird. From that point on, the action just kept getting better. Birds zoomed into the area looking to sit down. We worked a pair of mallards. Close, but no cigar. Then a flock of green-wings actually made it into the blocks before we realized it. I took one on the rise but Justin had difficulty picking them out of the dark shadows of the trees so he held his fire — that's a lot of maturity for a twelve year old. We went through quite a few shells that morning as I deferred to my son and then tried to down escapees when things didn't necessarily work out. In the end, we had a game bag full of woodies, teal, mallards and blacks. We also ended up being in the most productive spot on the lake. We had as much action as the other three parties combined in what was my last resort to save the day. Oh well, you know the old saying, "I'd rather be lucky than good any day!"

CHAPTER 10

Westward Ho for Wapiti

We'd been climbing straight up for nearly twenty minutes and I was sucking every molecule of oxygen I could into my lungs. When I say we were going straight up it's no exaggeration. We were grabbing brush, roots and rocks pulling ourselves up into the heart of the Rocky Mountains. The bull we were chasing had topped the first ridge long ago; we could only hope and pray that he would pull up and give us a chance to catch him. My guide, Lance, and I had bumped into the bull before first light, after wading the White River in the dark and entering a canyon locally known as Hell's Hip Pocket. We got him talking to us, but he had cows with him and decided to take them and head into the high country after a cow blew us in on our second setup. It was early in my first weeklong bow hunt for elk and I was damn glad that I had taken my adventure to the Colorado Rockies seriously and worked out all summer in preparation for it. Being a nearly lifelong resident of upstate New York, I knew well-conditioned lungs and legs would be imperative in order for me to have any chance at all of harvesting my first elk. I had read enough magazine articles and watched a sufficient number of videos to know that physical conditioning was an integral part of elk hunting.

I've traveled all over the United States and have explained numerous times that all of New York is not skyscrapers and pavement. Actually, that couldn't be further from the truth. I live smack dab in the center of the Empire State where farm fields, forests and brush lots weave a pastoral tapestry between small towns and villages. Rolling hills, small streams and lakes are home to whitetails, turkeys, black bear, otters, beaver and waterfowl of all types. This countryside even supported herds of elk when settlers arrived here a couple of centuries ago. And if everything goes well and the Rocky Mountain Elk Foundation is successful, we may hear the bugles of bulls and the chirps of cows in the not too distant future. But even with all this, central New York State is a world apart from the Continental Divide. On training runs through my woods, I'd be lucky to gain two hundred feet in elevation. During one morning of my elk hunt, I hiked ten miles and gained two *thousand* feet in elevation and the only elk talk I heard back home was the echoing of my own feeble attempts at sounding like a big bull. Even though I didn't live in the middle of elk country, I was prepared to tackle the landscape that they inhabit. And I sure wasn't in New York anymore.

I must admit however, that when I pulled into camp and started to acquaint myself with the other hunters, some of whom had been there for awhile, I was a little unsure whether I was ready or not. I was talking with a fellow from North Carolina, who'd been hiking the mountains chasing elk with his compound bow for a couple of days, as I placed my gear into a fairly large day pack in preparation for my first day afield. As we discussed hunting in the mountains he got a wry smile on his face and said in a smooth southern drawl, "You won't be toting that thing along after the first day. I started out with a pack like that and now I'm down to this," at which point he held up what looked like a wallet and water bottle. Needless to say, he hadn't prepared himself for the ruggedness of the mountains and the altitude. And he sure wasn't in North Carolina anymore either.

All this being said, there is always the other side of the coin. Also in camp on my first day was a gent from Michigan who had hunted there the year before. Dick was not a young man and to say that he was big would be an understatement. He was overweight, to put it politely, and had bad legs, too. Go figure! There was no way he was going to move through any of this country without great difficulty, but damned if he hadn't killed a bull elk the previous year and was now back to get another. He had just arrived in his pickup truck after driving half way across the country in a couple of days. Dick had only been in camp an hour or two when one of the guides gathered him up and headed down the road to get an elk. The rest of the tale goes like this. They traveled to a relatively flat piece of elk country, parked the truck, ventured no more than three hundred yards off a gravel road and started bugling trying to locate a bull. They immediately had one bugle back at them and start to move in their direction. To make a long story short, the bull ended up coming right in, and ol' Dick from Michigan got at arrow into him and put him down for the count. Upon his return to camp that evening Dick let us know that this elk hunting was just way too easy and he was going back to Michigan to chase whitetails. I must admit that the man did make lethal shots on two bull elk. Unfortunately, though, ol' Dick had absolutely no appreciation for God's country or the noble animals, which he had successfully harvested. But that's hunting, even elk hunting.

Even though Lance and I didn't have another encounter with that 5x5 we chased up the mountain, I was already being rewarded by the magnificence of the animal and the habitat it now calls home. That little jaunt up the mountainside was in complete contrast to sitting in the woods back home waiting for a one hundred and fifty pound whitetail buck to pass underneath my treestand. The bull we were pursuing looked as big as a horse. And how he ran up that slope as quickly and quietly as he did was beyond my comprehension. It was especially hard to fathom, considering that he was carrying a huge rack atop his head, which lie along his back, as he maneuvered through the trees and oak brush.

Lance and I continued up the mountain crossing huge parks, cutting through ravines and wending our way through groves of aspen. I continually stopped to admire the majestic vistas and deeply inhale the cool mountain air laced with the pungent aroma of sagebrush. As far as I was concerned, I was, once again, in heaven. Traipsing through the mountains chasing elk with a recurve bow in my hand was only a dream a few short years before. Even though we Easterners can many times go hunting in our own backyards we're pretty much limited to pursuing whitetails. So, we spend a lot of time dreaming about the Rocky Mountain west where it's possible to hunt antelope, mule deer, bear, cougar and elk all in the same year if you have the hankering. And frankly, we're envious of those who can do just that.

My first encounter with a bull wapiti was memorable to say the least but it was time to get back after them. Midway through my hunt, after seeing numerous elk and putting scores of miles on my hiking boots, Lance and I checked out a large meadow situated in a creek bottom as the sun began to sink below the western ridgeline. After sneaking to the edge of the trees, we spotted several cows and calves grazing on the sweet grasses and forbs of early autumn. Glassing the area we spotted a decent 6x6 breaking out of the cover just a couple of hundred yards away. Lance challenged the bull, which immediately took the bait. We made a hasty plan and got set up as my quarry approached. Coming to the edge of the trees fifty yards away, the herd bull started to put on a show. Bugling furiously, saliva dripping from his mouth, he wasn't going to allow his "adversary" to take one of his girls. Lance attempted to rile him up again but try as we might, he wouldn't budge from the perimeter of the woods. He kept up the show by demolishing a small tree, throwing branches, leaves, dirt and sod several yards around him as the day started to fade to black. Unfortunately, I had set up on the down-slope side of Lance. Had I set up above him I would have had a chance at the bull given the fact that he came in wanting the uphill advantage. And if I'd had a little more experience at this game, I would have made a move on him as he rearranged the shrubbery at the edge of the meadow. But I didn't, so all I could do is watch as the victor joined his harem and grazed off into the twilight.

After seeing dozens of elk over the next couple of days with no real opportunity at taking any of them, my hunt was fast approaching its end. Fortuitously though, we had discovered a hotspot where we were continually getting into something, so on the evening of day six we ventured there to see what we might scare up. Hiking up a moderate slope below the crest of a mountain we immediately got into elk. Unfortunately, we had yet to make it to the timber just a short jaunt away. A calf lingered on the ridge above us and was soon joined by a cow. Lance and I started to do a little cow talk as things started to quickly fall into place. The cow and calf began to move down the slope toward us when we heard even more hoof beats coming from the same direction through the talus. Lance and I hit the dirt with little cover around to hide in. A half a dozen cows and calves passed by me at twenty yards or so. Watching them as they went by, I heard another elk moving in our direction. This time it was a bull.

He was coming in a hurry and was going to cruise right by me as he traced the path of the cows and calves. The bull was not big; he was what most elk hunters would call a rag-horn. This meant that I had to make sure that he was a shooter, since he needed to have a minimum of four points on at least one side of his rack. As he closed the distance between us I started counting — one, two, three, I can't shoot him; one, two, three, nope not enough; one, two, three — frantically I searched for a fourth point as I raised up on my knees bringing the bow up preparing to draw. Just as the bull passed in front of me, Lance bugled, stopping him in his tracks. But what could I do? I couldn't shoot; he wasn't legal. Then Lance said, "Shoot, shoot!" Shoot? What's he talking about, I wondered. Then it all fell apart, with the bull taking off to follow the rest of the small herd as Lance asked me why in hell I didn't shoot him. Unbeknownst to me, the bull was legal — he had three points on his right side, which I was counting, but four on his left, which Lance was counting. It all happened so fast I just never looked at the other half of his rack. There went an excellent opportunity, not at a big bull mind you, but that was of no consequence to me.

At this point in the hunt, I had come to realize that Lance had a sixth sense about elk. Many hunters develop this type of uncanny ability once they get to know their prey intimately. After discussing my miscue and kicking the dirt a little, we headed up the mountain to see what we might get into before dark. Hiking up through the timber we broke out into a huge meadow and walked along its edge. Having gone several hundred yards, Lance stopped abruptly and eased into the trees. The spot seemed to be no different than any other along the way, but as we entered the timber Lance froze! I was a couple of steps behind him when he raised his hand and pointed out in front of him. All week long, this simple gesture meant that I should carefully move forward but regrettably, it didn't mean that at this point. I began to sneak up into position causing several large animals to bust their way through the trees and brush and hightail it to parts unknown. Unbelievably, we had cut into the black timber precisely where our friend, the 3x4 bull, ended up with his small harem. And yet again, I had blown a good chance: He had been no more than ten yards in front of us.

We gave chase to several more bulls over the course of the next two days but never got close enough to attempt a shot. My initial quest for elk was over and I had never even drawn my bow. Again, that's hunting! I had literally hiked miles and miles through the western spine of our great nation chasing elk without ever decreasing the size of my pack, I might add. I had seen all manner of game including mule deer, whitetails and moose. And even though I never loosed an arrow, I had developed a deep appreciation for my quarry and the country where it now resides, so much so that I left Colorado with an immediate longing to return in my search for elk.

CHAPTER 11

Doggin' After Grouse

I was ripping my way through the middle of the thick stuff, you know, the hearty mix of alder brush, blackberry canes, thorn apple and the like that no sane person ventures into voluntarily — the kind of cover we affectionately call junk, as in, "Who's going through the junk?" It had been my turn to dive in and I finally hit a small clearing and stopped, waiting for something to happen. After pausing to catch my breath and make sure I wasn't bleeding profusely, I took a few tentative steps assessing where to plow through the jungle between the woods and me. At that moment, my brother Bob yelled "BIRD!" My body stiffened in preparation to throw the gun to my shoulder, as my eyes scanned the cover to the west awaiting the emergence of my intended target. Suddenly the bird made the edge, revealing itself to me for what seemed like only a nanosecond, higher and further away then expected. The pump gun came up as if under its own power and my trigger finger convulsed, sending a load of lead pellets skyward. The fan-tailed rocket flinched and a few feathers were left in its wake as it made the tall hemlocks to the east. I marked its flight line as Gina, my tried and true hunting dog, materialized from the thicket where the grouse originated. Our paths merged and together we headed off in the direction the bird had taken.

Being a knowledgeable, experienced grouse hunter, I had my distinct opinions as to the destiny of the bird. So, I guided Gina to where I thought we would either find the bird lying on the forest floor or put it up for another shot opportunity. We combed the area thoroughly but to no avail. There was no sign of a ruffed grouse either dead or alive. As Bob and the rest of my hunting party joined us, we ambled off, giving up our search for the bird. Hitting an old railroad bed, we walked together discussing the morning's events and made plans as to what our next move would be. Gina hadn't come out with us so I stopped from time to time calling for her to join us so that we could get on with the hunt. We had been out of the woods for some time and still the dog had yet to show. Slowly shuffling along, I began to worry a bit about Gina's whereabouts; this wasn't like her. I turned again not only to call her but also to start back and see if I could find her. As I did, she topped the railroad grade in full stride with a bird in her mouth. Somehow, she knew the grouse was down and found it, so much for my knowledge, skills and abilities!

I've hunted ruffed grouse with and without dogs, mostly with though. And there is nothing better than a canine that knows its way around the grouse woods. Now I don't want to give anyone the impression that I have brought up and heartily trained my dogs to hunt grouse. I have raised a number of bird dogs but my training program has been nothing more than to get the dogs out in the fields and forests as young and as often as possible. The main things I've worked on with these dogs is coming when called, staying close in the field and tunneling through the junk to find game, because what I want from a bird dog is for it to find, flush and retrieve birds for me. However, after a hunter and dog have spent numerous days afield together, the relationship is much more than gun toting hunter and working dog: The two become a team. A turn by one causes the other to veer. As one pauses, it elicits the other to hesitate. A retrace of the trail induces the other to back track. I consider myself fortunate in having developed this spirit of teamwork with several of my canine companions.

Another springer spaniel of mine, Abby, was a true testament to teamwork. She has, to this point, been the best grouse dog I have ever spent the day with in a grouse covert. This is probably a direct result of the fact that I have spent more time in the field with her than any other dog I have ever owned. Abby and I had hunted a little corner woods several times one particular fall in hopes of adding a bird to our bag. The woodlot was not the best grouse habitat in the world but populations were high at the time and we could usually count on a flush or two. Each time we had pursued birds there in the past they always found a way to elude us. Usually they'd sneak out a side door and seek safe haven in a big woods managed by the county, where hunting was prohibited. Smart birds!

It was on a typically crisp, clear autumn day that Abby and I found ourselves at the place where success was yet to be had. Instead of transecting the cover, as we had in the past, I decided to circle around on the outside edge and set up at one of the most commonly used escape routes. Abby accompanied me, avoiding entry into the woods and notification of our presence. A huge, old hemlock stood guard at one of our quarry's most utilized portals, so I decided to stand with it and send Abby into the brush to see what she might find. First, I watched her, and then listened as she thoroughly worked the cover in search of our prey. She knew exactly what the strategy was and looped far out in front of me, and then started back straight for me. I had never said a word, just signaled to her to go in and find something. Suddenly a bird flushed, as only a grouse can do, and headed right for my lookout post. Like a shot at station number eight of a skeet range, my gun went up and traced the bird's path to its zenith. As the end of the barrel blotted out its silhouette, I yanked the trigger resulting in a plume of feathers and the plummet of the partridge back to Mother Earth. The dog arrived as the bird hit the ground and gleefully picked it up and brought it to hand. It doesn't get any better than that! And take it from me; this was no isolated incident. Abby, on numerous occasions, has used a circuitous route to put birds right in my lap, so much so that there is no way it happened by chance.

Hunting with a good dog is more than a pleasurable experience — it has numerous benefits, not the least of which is peace of mind. It's one thing to have confidence in a dog's ability to find and flush game, it's quite another to know that your companion can and will come up with downed birds. After all these years traversing fields and forests, swamps and mountains, I have come to know the exhilaration of success, however measured, as well as the frustration of defeat. However, there is no worse feeling in hunting than knowing you have mortally wounded a wild creature and not been able to claim and utilize it. In these instances, dogs that tirelessly search for cloistered game are, as they say, worth their weight in gold!

During a peak grouse year in the late 80s, I was on a good run, hunting often and adding fresh grouse breasts to our weekly menu. I had two very good dogs at the time and often hunted them together when going out by myself. But when accompanied by another hunter I usually worked with one dog to limit any confusion on the dog's part and mine. It was just easier. Tracie, my German shorthair, could find the only bird inhabiting a square mile if given the opportunity. She was, as most German shorthairs are, sleek and single-minded. Her only shortcoming was once a bird was down and dead she could care less. No matter how much I worked with her, she never could be counted on to find a bird that had been knocked down. She was Abby's teammate and together they were unbeatable as far as I was concerned. Tracie was an unflagging courser and Abby an assiduous retriever. Throughout our lives together, their abilities never ceased to amaze me.

I had agreed to take my next-door neighbor, Jim, out on a little walk one Saturday afternoon that fall to pursue grouse and woodcock. Always one to want to show people my abilities afield, I planned to hunt one of my favorite honey holes where I could almost guarantee at least a modicum of action. As I prepared to leave the house, my intentions were to take Tracie along and leave Abby at home. Whoever was left behind was going to raise holy hell, whining and pacing incessantly looking for any chance to escape the confines of the house in order to go hunting. But for some reason, still not readily apparent to me, I changed my mind and gave Abby the nod. Maybe it was the fact that I had, days earlier, taken Tracie on a very successful pheasant hunt, or maybe it was a premonition, I'm not sure. In the end, it was Tracie having the conniption.

Abby and I joined up with Jim and headed off to complete a circuit through the grouse woods. We hadn't been out long when we approached an area that was more likely to produce a timber-doodle than a partridge. With cover running thin, Abby dove into a brush pile and out came a grouse rocketing straight away. My gun started up but I deferred to Jim, planning to back him up if he missed. He did not! Feathers flew everywhere and the grouse nose-dived to the ground. I congratulated him on a fine shot as we went to meet Abby at the bird's landing spot. However, as she went to pick Jim's harvest up, an avian bomb exploded, taking flight from underneath our feet and catching all of us off guard. And after reaching cruising altitude, the bird glided a couple of hundred yards ditching into a thick stand of spruce trees. What the heck? Was that a second grouse? It certainly couldn't have been the bird Jim had downed. But after searching for quite awhile, and knowing what we had witnessed, we came to the only conclusion we could reach. The bird that Jim had shot got up and flew away. God knows how many grouse I have hit and seen hit before and since, but it's a lot and I have never seen anything like that.

The bird had gone into a plantation of young trees many acres in size and thicker than hair on a dog's back. I decided we should continue to hunt, carefully marking where it entered the grove so that we could check it out on the way home. We forged onward put-ting out a few more grouse and adding a woodcock to our game bag. With evening bearing down on us, we decided to check on the fate of Jim's bird before heading home. We hugged the edge of the spruce reforestation with Abby, who led the way, stopping occa-sionally to sniff at this and that. Nearing the spot where we saw the partridge cut in, Abby stopped, smelled the air, then doubled back and entered the green needled-jungle. Jim and I backed off, not knowing what to expect. In no time at all though, Abby sprang out, proud as a peacock with the bird cradled securely between her jaws. I never would have believed it if I hadn't seen it with my own eyes. That grouse was mortally wounded, hit the ground, then got up and flew the equivalent of two football fields before succumbing, very atypical for ruffed grouse. Thank God for great bird dogs!

CHAPTER 12

A Buck for Justin

In the autumn of 1998 I had recently completed a yearlong stint in Washington D.C. as a Congressional Fellow working for the U.S. Senate Committee on Agriculture, Nutrition and Forestry. I was involved in policy formulation related to natural resource conservation issues. The work was interesting, enlightening and rewarding but being away from home, I found out, was not my cup of tea. It also brought into focus how meaningful it is to share time, and experiences, with my family and how important they are to me. In fact, the time away had a huge impact on me and has actually changed the course of my life. This story relates my return home to my family and some of the most valued things in life.

Over the preceding few years, Justin, who was ten years old at the time, had become increasingly interested in bowhunting. He'd been shooting a longbow since he was seven and had recently started to participate in 3-D shoots with me. During the fall of '97, he even sat in a treestand next to mine a couple of times during the archery season. Unfortunately, that's about all the hunting we did since I was working three hundred and eighty miles from home. Hopefully, that won't happen again! Upon my return to a more normal routine, Justin and I couldn't wait for bowhunting season to start. He knew of course, that he could only accompany me when he didn't have other obligations like school and extracurricular activities. Justin really longed to be there if everything came together, but even if he wasn't, he wanted me to get a deer almost as much as I did. So, on the first Saturday of the season, he jumped out of bed ready to head to the woods with his dad. I'll let Justin tell you what happened that day. His words convey his excitement and enthusiasm better than any I could write to describe it.

"The first thing we did was get up real early (5 a.m.). We got all of our hunting clothes on and went outside to get my dad's bow. After that we stepped into the woods and the hunt began! As we were walking, we heard deer shuffling through the leaves. We stopped every so often to listen for deer. Once we stopped after hearing some deer. My dad said someone was following us, but he was just joking. By the way, we had to whisper!

After we were done walking we climbed into our treestands. After a short time, Dad spotted movement in the brush. It was a deer! The problem was we couldn't tell whether it was a buck or doe. At the same time, there was a doe right behind us! This was awesome!

Later I was looking around for deer, and then all of a sudden I saw one. It moved and I saw that it was a buck. An eight-point buck! He veered off to my left into the brush. Dad told me to grunt at him with the call he had given me after we had gotten into our stands. So I did. Suddenly the eight-point came back looking for the other buck, which was really me! He almost came in for a shot, but ran off around some apple trees and to the right of us. Then we saw something awesome, he made a scrape! Then he went farther to our right but never quite came close enough for *us* to shoot! Later we got down to look at the buck's scrape and on our way, we saw two other scrapes. It couldn't have been a better setup!"

I was looking for everything to work out to build on our hunting memories together. We went to the woods several more times and saw deer each time, but things hadn't worked out as I had hoped. During my solitary forays into the woods, I saw numerous bucks and had several "almost" situations, including a close encounter of the Pope and Young kind. But that's another story.

All of this laid the groundwork for the events that were about to transpire on that warm October afternoon. The wind had been squirrelly all day and I had thought, more than once, about abandoning the hunt but something in my heart told me to stay put and enjoy the evening. About an hour before quitting time, a flash of deer hide caught my attention. After several minutes of studying the shadowy figure through the dense undergrowth, I determined that the deer was a buck. Not a big buck, but quite honestly I'm not all that choosy. He didn't appear to be coming my way at first. I figured he'd make a beeline to the meadow I was sitting near, never affording me a shot.

The buck was in no hurry and loitered in the thick stuff nosing the ground, occasionally looking toward the wide-open spaces of the hayfield. A short time later, he picked up his head and started right for me, angling back into the woods. Now I presumed he wasn't going to the meadow at all, but was just checking the area for does. Due to this thorough understanding of deer behavior, I was still seated in my stand. Not a good position to be in when your quarry is about to offer you a shot opportunity. Since I shoot a stick bow, I prefer a standing shot out of a treestand. I can shoot from a sitting position, but I'm not comfortable doing it. At any rate, this buck was headed toward me and I had no choice but to sit tight where I was. Obviously, I should have eased up as soon as I saw him but I didn't. He ended up transecting the trail I was hunting over and made a left hand turn onto it, headed straight for me. The finely antlered devil passed quickly through my first shooting lane, then the second. He finally stopped in the third and last hole through the brush. This presented me with a shot where I had to turn as far as I could to my right. A tough maneuver for a right handed shooter in a seated position. I picked a spot behind his shoulder and let the arrow go.

The shot was only ten yards and it should have been perfect, but it wasn't. No matter how much visualization you go through, things don't always come to pass the way they ought to. The arrow struck the deer just behind the rib cage angling back and through his body. Instinctively the buck took off on a dead run, retreating in the direction he had come from. I could only monitor his exodus for the first thirty to forty yards until the mixed northern hardwood forest swallowed him up. Given the shot, I quickly decided that I would sneak away and wait out the situation overnight. Any effort to locate the buck that evening would have been fruitless. My mind raced through all the possibilities, finally settling on the scenario that the buck would head downhill, toward thick cover adjacent to the creek, where he would bed down and expire. I had to come to this conclusion, since it was the best possible outcome.

I returned at dawn with Darren, who graciously took time off from work to assist me in finding my buck. Upon close examination, we found that the blood trail was anything but profuse. The deer had angled uphill on a well-used trail. This fact didn't do much for my optimism. Darren and I employed the old arrow in the ground method to mark the trail, using two arrows to leap frog the sign as we went. After fifty yards or so, the blood trail diminished to a spot here and a splat there. In our attempt to work it out Darren and I got confused. It seemed as though we were working two different trails, because we didn't have anything to look back on for a reference. At that point, I thought, wait a minute, the evidence is here, and we're just not dealing with it properly. So, I rummaged through my pack to retrieve a roll of fluorescent orange surveyor's tape, a move I should have made at the outset of our search!

I went back to square one while Darren went uphill, to known bedding areas, to look around. Starting ten yards from my stand, I started to flag the trail. Unfortunately, I could only go so far due to the minimal sign. I then went to where we had been working the "second" trail and marked it as far as I could. It was at that point that the puzzle came together. I found a speck of blood on a leaf two feet above the ground. The buck had started uphill, going eighty yards or so. At that point, I assume it realized that it was hurt, then turned and headed straight downhill toward the creek bottom. Darren had returned from his inquisitive poking around, empty-handed, to tell me he had to leave for work. He bid me adieu and wished me luck. I wished me luck too! My hopes were raised as I took up the trail again working it along the creek for another sixty to seventy yards. Sign was scant at that point and I looked and looked but found nothing. The well had gone dry. I thought back to my best-case scenario and decided to take a little walk to an area I was familiar with due to my scouting trips with Justin.

I knew of a small swampy area, just off the creek, approximately two hundred yards from where the blood trail had petered out. Off I went! After searching the area thoroughly and turning up nothing, I decided to walk the creek downstream a ways peering into the alder and willow tangles as I slowly proceeded. All I had was faith and a feeling in my gut that this is where the buck had ended up. Having gone approximately fifty yards, I concluded that I should wade the creek bottom back upstream just to make sure I thoroughly scrutinized the entire area, so, into the water I went. As I approached a narrow finger of cattails, I heard what sounded like stones rolling down the creek bank. It couldn't be my buck digging out of there, could it? It had been hours since he was hit! The noise prompted me to crawl up out of the creek and survey the landscape. After picking my way through the brush I spied a patch of blackberries that I had previously walked right past. This was the kind of spot a wounded deer might seek out to hole up in. I walked half way around that little patch and there he lie, having succumbed to the keen sharpness of my broadhead tipped cedar shaft. What the noise was I'll never know. Maybe it was a sign from the hunting gods!

The evening I shot the deer, I had told Justin about what had happened. I even considered letting him miss school and accompany me to find my buck, but I thought better of it. Luckily, I beat him home from school that day. He couldn't wait to get there and learn of my success (or failure) in finding our trophy. Justin was ecstatic as I dropped the tailgate of my truck to reveal the little six-pointer, a deer that he had seen on one of our outings to scout the area. Things had worked out! I had taken a buck from a treestand that my son helped me put up and from an area we had scouted together. Unfortunately, Justin wasn't with me when the deer was harvested. But I know that he was happy for me and he'll always have vivid memories of the buck dad got for him!

CHAPTER 13

I'll Be Danged

The hot, humid summer days were finally starting to wane and my thoughts were turning more and more to the fall ahead. This was to be no ordinary autumn. Justin had turned twelve shortly after the summer solstice and received a new 20 gauge shotgun for his birthday. With his prerequisite hunter safety course behind him, the young lad was more than ready for his first opportunity to chase wild creatures in the great outdoors. Normally, I'm totally focused on preparing for the bow season at this time of year. Bowhunting is an endeavor that tends to be all consuming to many and I include myself in those ranks. Due to this affliction, my scouring the woods for grouse, fields for pheasants, and lakes, marshes, swamps, and rivers for ducks has been significantly diminished in recent years. My son's ever increasing interest in pursuit of these wild fowl however, was fanning the embers of my own fires to get back to my roots in hunting. As the days grew shorter and cool breezes blew in from the northwest, I worked with Justin to hone his shotgunning skills. First, we shot at clay pigeons hung on dead trees out in our woods. After mastering his stance, shooting with both eyes open and smoothly bringing the gun up to his shoulder, we decided to see if he could hit more evasive targets. We took several trips to our local rod and gun club to shoot clay birds launched from my trusty old Trius trap thrower. Every time we went, Justin's percentage would increase as he learned the basics of swinging with his target and following through.

I had decided that my boy's first hunt would occur on Youth Day for young duck hunters. This presented an absolutely great opportunity for the youngsters of our state to go afield and dip their toes into the wonderful world of waterfowling, both figuratively and literally. As the day approached, Justin and I collected the necessary provisions that would hopefully make our day a productive one. Waders, steel shotshells, gun, decoys and camouflage face paint were ready to be loaded into the truck a few days prior to opening morning. Then it crossed my mind: Justin had never taken more than a single shot at a time with his downsized pump gun. More seasoned duck hunters know that having three shells in the gun is not only comforting, but also presents opportunity, and in some cases erases the sin of missing with the first shot. So, the evening before our hunt Justin and I made a quick trip to the range to get in a little more practice.

With a few warm-up targets under his belt, Justin was breaking eighty percent of those launched and I told him I would put two birds on the thrower. I also explained to him that whether or not he broke either of them was immaterial, I just wanted him to get the feel of having more than one shell in the gun, pumping the forearm and firing successive shots. Justin nodded his head, affirming his readiness, so I pulled the cord on the trap and the two clay birds sailed away into the azure, autumn sky. As might be expected Justin broke the first clay; and after pumping the gun and searching for the second one, shot at it as it lit into the brush, totally unscathed. He handled himself well and eagerly requested a second chance. Once again, two shells went into the gun and two birds went on the thrower. After checking his stance, he focused his attention to the eventual flight path of his "quarry" and yelled, "Pull!" Again, the clay pigeons lifted toward the heavens. At the first report of his gun, one of the birds disappeared in a cloud of black and orange dust. This time Justin was more expedient in pumping his gun and locating the second target. Boom, the second bird fragmented into several pieces and fell toward earth. I just stood there and shook my head: I'll be danged; my son broke a double on his second attempt! Half a box of shells later, it was apparent that he was not only ready and willing, but also able for his first day afield.

The weather on the kids' opener couldn't have been more perfect. The day dawned with cool temperatures, partly cloudy skies and a stiff wind out of the north — conditions that would work very well for the temporary brush blind that I had built a few days earlier on the upstream end of a fairly large lake. With legal shooting time fast approaching, Justin and I found ourselves anxiously waiting for the whirring of wings toward our modest, albeit inviting setup. Given the fact that it was Youth Day, Justin was the only one toting a gun to the blind that morning. My job was to watch for birds, work the duck call and coach as best I could. The funny thing is I don't remember the sheer joy of a hunt more than that which I experienced that day, even though I was not shooting a gun. I checked and rechecked my watch; the long awaited hour had finally come.

No more did we load Justin's gun and review safety measures one last time than the first birds started working our blocks. The first twenty minutes were intense. Puddle ducks of all sorts were buzzing overhead and careening past our blind, some of which snuck in low to land in our decoys. Justin went though a fistful of shells, but to that point, not a feather had been touched. This was a whole different deal than shooting at clay birds. The activity slowed a bit as the day grew brighter and we began working singles, doubles, and small flocks looking for that first bird to come to hand. It wasn't long before three birds spied our "ducks" and swung in from the west. As they approached, I identified them as mallards and whispered to Justin to hold tight until the first duck was about to touch down. A drake and his hen sliced over the blocks and looked to set down just out of good gun range. Justin quickly turned his attention to the third bird, which lagged behind a bit. The greenhead cupped his iridescent wings and lowered his bright orange landing gear to set down in the hole between his artificial buddies. Justin jumped up, threw the gun to his shoulder and pulled the trigger. The bird crumpled and splashed into the murky water, lying totally still except for the motion imparted by its liquid resting place. "I got him!" Justin exclaimed. I grabbed my boy like only a dad can do to his son, and gave him a big hug, then exited the blind to retrieve his first duck. Justin was thrilled! Returning to his side, we examined the juvenile bird, straightening its feathers and reviewing basic identification keys. There is nothing like a modicum of success to bring out the exuberance in a young man, or anyone for that matter, and Justin was now talking up a storm with a duck in the bag! The sun was just starting to peek over the hills behind us so I grabbed up my camera and snapped a few pictures for posterity.

After our brief photo session, and a few near misses, the action slowed appreciably and Justin and I talked of the hunt and the thrill of downing his inaugural bird. I guess we weren't paying complete attention to the skies around us because out of the corner of my eye a bird caught my attention as it glided into the decoys to join its "friends." The drake widgeon was well within range and I told Justin to be ready when we stood up, as the bird would lift off and take flight. However, because it was early in the season and the bird was immature, it held tight so I stood totally erect and let out a yell. Hearing me bellow, the bird quickly got up. Justin was premature with the first shot. As I watched the pattern splash into the water, it was obvious that the shot was low and left. Before I could utter a word though, Justin pumped his gun and squeezed off a second round. The bird folded and fell to earth on a small island of water worked rocks. A huge smile grew on my face and all I could say was, "I'll be danged!" I couldn't believe how focused and smooth Justin was. That was pretty impressive, and not really expected from my young, inexperienced protégé.

A fortnight had gone by when Justin and I found ourselves looking over new water. Lake Moraine had been the scene of numerous canoe and fishing outings over the past few years, but I had never ventured there to pursue waterfowl. Due to the evident hunting pressure, Justin and I paddled through the still darkness of opening morning to a backwater bay nestled in among a grove of hemlocks. I wasn't sure what the morning would bring as we picked a likely spot along shore to put in and set out a few decoys. Our work was done in short order, so Justin and I sat high and dry among the trees to wait for legal shooting light. I was able to play a more active role on this trip so I had my reliable pump gun along to assist with the task at hand. We shuffled our way into a thicket of shallow water cattails as the appointed hour arrived. After double-checking our watches, we heard the morning's first shots out on the open water; further indicating it was time to load up. We continued to get ready, clearing cattails out of our shooting lanes and checking for good footing. Nothing makes for good marksmanship more than clear shooting paths and a stable stance.

We had just gotten settled in and started to scan the sky for signs of beating wings when several birds started to swing our way out of the dimly lit northern sky. Flight pattern and whistling voices clued us in that they were woodies as they rapidly closed the distance between us. The birds looked as though they would fly right over us and set down on the far end of the small bay we were hunting. As they approached, I told Justin to get ready as this was going to come together in a hurry. When they were forty-five degrees above the horizon I yelled, "Take 'em!" Our guns, now pointing toward the zenith, blazed in the dawn's early light as they passed directly overhead. The birds had come in fast and hard, and at a shooting angle that's as tough for a veteran as it is for a novice. Only two shots were fired, one from my 12 gauge and one from Justin's 20. The report of our guns reverberated off the forested fortress surrounding us as my wood duck was falling to the water, closely followed by Justin's. Again, all I could say was "I'll be danged!" What a moment. We had accomplished a perfect father-son double that will be indelibly etched in my mind for the rest of my days on earth. When we retrieved our birds, we discovered that I had taken a beautiful mature drake and Justin a very nice mature hen, a fitting result given our relative tenures in the marsh. It didn't take us long to decide that these two birds would grace our walls at home, not only because they were perfect specimens, but more importantly to further commemorate our time together.

Justin's one of those people that when they decide to do something they go after it with great interest and zeal. He was now a died-in-the-wool duck hunter and I'm sure he'll have more surprises in store for me. More surprises and more opportunities for me to exclaim "I'll be danged!"

CHAPTER 14

My Odyssey

The season had been a struggle for the first two weeks. I had hunted hard but saw little, especially as far as bucks were concerned. Warm weather, competing hunters and a busy schedule acted as obstacles as I pursued my antlered objective. And, as often happens, I wasn't seeing anything from the same stands that I had hunted the year before when I was almost beating away bucks with a stick! That fact frustrated me even more. The weather had finally turned colder though and it just felt more like deer hunting so I was hopeful about my morning hunt as I tiptoed down the stairs to prepare for yet another outing.

I took up my usual predawn rituals of showering, retrieving my clothes from an odor proof bag and donning my camouflage duds before heading out the door with my recurve bow. But before I could go, I needed to find my Glo-Mitts. These glove-mitten combinations were essential now that the temperatures had dipped. Unfortunately, they weren't where I thought I had left them, so the search was on. To this point, everything had been going according to design and I had left myself plenty of time to get to my stand without hurrying. Now that my hand wear was missing, the seconds were ticking away and my ransacking of the house became increasingly frantic.

I looked high and low and in the process found my lucky rope, which had been missing in action since the season began. I thought I had lost it in the woods while placing my stands. Eureka, there it was hiding under a piece of furniture. I'm not sure that the piece of rope is all that lucky but an old friend gave it to me a long time ago and I took a nice eight-point buck the same day. It has been a prized possession ever since. That length of braided hemp has been used to haul up stands, pull down rogue tree limbs, drag out deer and, in emergencies, even used as a safety belt, so when I couldn't find it at the beginning of the hunting season I was bummed. It actually had been eating at me every time I went to the woods. This was due more to the fact that I couldn't find it, couldn't think of where I might have lost it, than its real intrinsic value or importance. I'm funny like that!

I was glad I had found my rope, but I still had nothing warm to protect my digits, so I grabbed my light knit gloves, my heavy camouflage coat, and bow and headed off to go hunting. My destination was a treestand that's, well, practically in my backyard. The great thing about it is that I can stalk the stand quietly and from downwind on a trail that I maintain through my property. As soon as I started walking across my lawn toward the woods, I heard deer bounding off. Not just a deer or two, it sounded like a whole damn herd. Unfortunately, this event is somewhat common, as the country that surrounds my house is prime deer habitat. Usually they'll run off perpendicular to my line of travel but that particular morning they just wanted to ruin a perfect approach to my stand and kept paralleling me, bumping more deer as we went. When I finally got to my stand, I was not in the best of moods to say the least! It was cold and I knew my hands wouldn't hold up long inside the lightweight gloves. And now it was later than I normally got in because I was looking for my Glo-Mitts and had to keep stopping to let the deer calm down. Plus, I had just pushed every deer within a half a mile radius off my property. Why even go up the tree? I'd had a good feeling about that morning's prospects when I crawled out of bed and by God, I was going to hunt no matter what! Before climbing up the tree, I went to put on my coat. That's when my luck started to turn. The heavy Glo-Mitts were stuffed up inside one of the sleeves of my coat. Yes! But who in the heck put them in there? Hmm! Up the tree I went, strapping in, almost certain I wouldn't see a thing. At least my hands would be warm! The woods had become solemnly quiet at last as I settled back to blend into my surroundings.

Long after the sun had risen over the hills in the east, a doe and two fawns worked their way toward me off a knoll that was cloaked in wild apple trees and located directly behind my stand. They were coming in on my right, so thinking a buck might follow, I got turned in that direction. This required me to move my bow quite a bit in order to get it to the opposite side of a tree that inhabits the space directly in front of my stand. After getting situated, I intently watched the doe and fawns as they fed below me. Hearing faint footfalls in back of me, I turned to spy a buck easing his way in my direction, but he was well above my hideout and not apt to present a shot opportunity. As he approached the other three deer, I feigned a bleat call. He immediately turned downhill toward the doe and fawns. The buck rushed toward them, like a bully in a schoolyard, causing them to dart in three different directions. The doe ended up on my left and behind me. One fawn found its way to a spot directly underneath me while the other, a button buck, took up following his significantly larger brethren. The small eight-pointer quickly walked through the only shooting lane I had, offering no shot, and stopped under an aging apple tree. Assuming he would continue to my left, I now had to raise my bow to get it on the other side of the tree where it was originally. It was now or never, as his attention was focused on the doe, so I made my move. The button buck stood right in front of me and watched intently as I maneuvered my bow around the obstacle. He ignored the movement and took up following the buck.

All four deer then stopped and stood there for what seemed like several minutes before the buck finally decided to give chase to the doe. He ended up nearly broadside, at nine yards, directly in front of me with nothing between us but the cool, crisp autumn air. After picking a "spot" behind his shoulder I went on auto pilot, a state of mind where you feel as though you're having an out of body experience and the bow seemingly takes on a life of its own. My Super Ghost recurve came to full draw as naturally as if I was pointing my finger at the buck. Before I knew it, the arrow had disappeared several feet beyond him into the leafy detritus on the ground. The buck bolted away, thirty yards or so, and stopped as the remainder of the small herd scattered.

The arrow hit him high, and back further than it should have, but the damage was lethal. The buck stood motionless for a long time, watching, listening, and smelling. As he did, I replayed the shot repeatedly in my mind. Why isn't he going down, I mused?

My mental gymnastics led me to the conclusion that the arrow went through the liver, but missed the all-important lungs. I then dauntingly realized that it was going to be a long day. The buck bedded down right where he had been standing and laid there for forty-five minutes, constantly alert for any intruders. He was situated so that he occasionally caught my wind, but he really couldn't react to it. I was not happy. I knew I wanted to get out of there if I could, but being in full view of the buck, I was pinned down. With the passing of each minute I started to worry about my family coming to look for me and spooking the buck out of there, since I was long overdue back at the house. Then he suddenly struggled to his feet, walked a few measured steps and bedded back down. It was obvious that he was in serious trouble but it was going to take a while for him to expire. Sometimes these are the vagaries of the hunt, like it or not, so all I could do is wait. Nearly an hour had passed and again the buck struggled to his feet. Unbelievably, he started to walk away, heading down off the small knoll where he had been lying. Now was my opportunity to sneak out of there. Given the hit, the buck's reaction and his condition I determined that it would be another four to six hours before I could take up the search. So, I slowly and quietly worked my way out of the area totally frustrated with the initial outcome of the day's events.

Back at the house, I phoned my good friend Walt Dixon. Walt is a longtime bowhunter, Deer Search member and all around good guy. His membership in Deer Search was the reason I contacted him. Deer Search is a volunteer organization whose members use specially trained tracking dogs to find wounded big game animals. At this point, I felt that I could use all the help I could get. We discussed the hit, the deer's actions and the impending strategy. I knew the deer was mortally wounded and there was no way I wouldn't ultimately find him. The power of positive thinking! Walt called me back mid-afternoon and we decided he would come over and we'd use his dogs to locate the buck. Walt has trailed many deer with his wirehaired dachshunds and I had the utmost confidence in their abilities, both his and the dogs. With the sun going down, Walt, Justin and I deliberately stalked the area where I last saw the buck and looked for any sign we might find. I recovered my arrow, minus its broadhead tipped end, and studied what little spore we found. Walt put his dogs to work, several times, but they didn't turn up much. The dogs use the odor of blood and bodily fluids to distinguish a wounded deer from a healthy one. Unfortunately, we just didn't have much to go on.

As the darkness of night started to close in upon us, I decided we should check an area some three hundred yards away. I had a feeling! A little voice in my head told me that the buck simply walked down off the hill, on a well-used snowmobile trail, crossed a narrow stretch of meadow and hid himself away in the alder brush adjacent to a small creek. I asked Walt to take the dogs upstream a ways and work his way slowly down the brush-choked waterway. Justin and I went downstream a quarter of a mile and started working back toward Walt and the dogs. No more than five minutes had ticked away when Walt yelled out indicating that he had busted a deer out of the thicket. The buck had indeed bedded down right next to the creek. On his last legs, the eight-point bolted up a steep, wooded hillside. I couldn't believe it. And it illustrated, once again, that deer are super tough animals. Walt got a dog on the trail and we started up after the buck. We walked less than a hundred yards and spotted him laying prostrate half way up the slope. My odyssey was over.

As a responsible bowhunter, I do my utmost to make every shot a perfect shot. But as every reasonable person knows, things don't always turn out the way we'd like them to. Fortunately, though, a razor sharp broadhead placed through the vitals of an animal will do its job. And if you stay calm, use your head and play your cards right things will work out in the end!

CHAPTER 15

Finger Lake Pheasants

The rolling hills of the Finger Lakes region of upstate New York are known for their pastoral beauty. Formed thousands of years ago by glaciers, first pushing southward out of today's Canada, then receding, leaving as their tracks a landscape comprised of gentle slopes bisected by long, narrow, deep lakes draining to the Atlantic Ocean through Lake Ontario and the St. Lawrence River. Over time, the vast hardwood forests, of maple, beech and hickory that covered the area, were utilized in building the foundation of a new found country; they were replaced by a patchwork of small family farms that eventually grew into one of the largest dairy industries in our nation's history. Many of those farms, along with their modest sized tractors and herds, have now disappeared and the countryside is gradually reverting back to the woodlands of old. In their wake, overgrown fields and stone-encumbered hedgerows provide excellent cover for a variety of wildlife species including the ring-necked pheasant. This bucolic scene provided the setting for a veteran bird hunter, his son and an old friend to pursue one of America's most beloved transplants.

It was the day after Thanksgiving and we had all stuffed ourselves, on what I consider one of my favorite family holidays, thus necessitating a little rest and relaxation on a frosty fall morning. It had snowed some over the preceding days and a frigid northwest breeze and low cloud cover guaranteed that the white, crystal-laden blanket would stick around yet another day. This was Justin's first year afield carrying a scattergun and my goal was to ensure that he had the opportunity to experience the idiosyncratic aspects of hunting waterfowl, ruffed grouse and pheasants during his rookie season. He had already gotten a full serving of ducks setting their wings in the decoys and a taste of chasing grouse around in old apple thickets, so we decided to team up with my buddy, Don and his English setter Mica, to complete Justin's trifecta, while burning off some of the thousands of calories consumed the previous day.

It was early afternoon by the time we had driven the two hours it took to get to our hunting location. The dog and Justin were eager to get into the field. Don and I on the other hand, were working the kinks out and deciding what exactly to wear, since it was cold out and the wind had kicked up some since our departure from home. However, the country we were hunting didn't have a flat spot in it so we decided to dress light and shiver for the first few minutes knowing full well the sweat would be rolling sooner rather than later. With our hunting garb selected, guns in hand and a bird dog raring to go, we strode down an old farm lane toward Justin's first pheasant hunt. No more had we gotten started when a bird flushed wildly out ahead of us and effortlessly glided hundreds of yards downhill into a brushy bottom. We'd pursue it later; there was an entire hillside to work with old fields and hedgerows aplenty. Proceeding up hill along either side of a wide field border, the strategy I had in mind was simple: Justin would get the honors, if at all possible, since he was new to the game. I would also defer to Don since it was his dog we were using and after having hunted with him before I knew there would be ample opportunity to back him up. That left me as the clean up man, directing strategy and making sure nothing got away. As we approached the end of the brush and weeds, a rooster got up in a vertical fashion, not unlike a helicopter, and turned with the wind to head straight down the slope. Four shots rang out in quick succession, with one providing a little more impetus for the bird to get moving, until he flew by me, at which time he folded at the report of my gun. Five spent shells, one bird and suddenly the cold stiff breeze and harsh crunch of winter's first snow felt perfect!

We had picked up a second bird out of a clump of trees before starting down a long, wide hedge with numerous brushy fence lines dead-ending into it — perfect cover for the wily birds. Mica had settled into a nice pace and worked the cover thoroughly with the wind fixed in her favor as we proceeded. Don was on the uphill side, Justin and I on the lower. Not only was I a father to the young lad walking along side of me, I was also his coach. I kept tabs on how he held his gun, how he walked and positioned himself and made sure he knew where everybody was, including the dog. It wasn't long before Mica froze into a classic point in a thick mass of brush, brambles and briars. As is the case more often than not, none of us could see the bird and it was decided that Don would go in after him. The bird, cackling vehemently, struggled out of the tangle and headed back between Don and Justin in the direction from which we had just come. Unlike the first two birds, I was a total spectator this time and eyed Justin as he hesitantly brought his gun up. It was as though he was checking and rechecking where everyone was before making a commitment — not a bad thing. His downsized 20 gauge finally found its place on his shoulder and he got off a quick shot. The rooster buckled and I started to bring my gun up, just in case. As good fortune would have it, it wasn't necessary. The raucous bird tumbled down in the thick stuff necessitating Mica's keen nose to help us find him. What a great moment, my son, with his first cock bird and me alongside to enjoy his youthful enthusiasm in a perfect setting. It really doesn't get any better than that!

After another close call and yet others that weren't, we neared the end of the long, pheasant harboring fencerow. Justin and I skittered along, side by side, locked in on Mica's movements or the

sound of her bell when she was out of sight. Approaching a break in the cover, we paused momentarily to let the dog work when a rooster exploded from underneath our feet. He went straight up over our heads before turning to fly to the bottom. I hit the ground while commanding Justin to shoot him. By the time he got situated the bird had kicked into high gear and Justin's single attempt at downing him passed harmlessly far behind his tail feathers. In a vain attempt to harvest the bird from my knees, I brought the gun up and slapped the trigger. He kept sailing away descending with the landscape to join the first rooster of the day in a jungle of thorn apple and blackberry canes.

Sometimes in order to get 'em you have to go in after them so, we hunted our way to the bottom. Don, Justin and I dove into the clot with great enthusiasm. It wasn't long though before our optimistic expectations drifted away like a small, downy feather on an autumn breeze. Perspiration was pouring off my brow and I was being stuck with needles and spines in all sorts of places. Justin ended up with a blackberry thorn embedded in the meaty part of his hand. After a little field surgery, and having covered several acres of the junk with no hint of a bird, we decided to get out of there and head upslope toward the ridge and more hospitable habitat. Walking along through cover we had already been through, a bird got up and headed bottomward. This time, however, it made a classic fishhook move and went into a small patch of woods. We went after it full bore, deciding to get below it and work up toward where we had seen it duck in. The plan worked perfectly. The bird flushed from its hideaway and again wanted to set its wings and soar down the hill. As it maneuvered through the trees, more akin to a grouse than a pheasant, Justin waited for it to clear the cover and, once it did, made an attempt at harvesting the bird. He missed however, and without hesitation, pumped another shell into the chamber and made a beautiful second shot.

With a fourth bird in the game bag, we decided to hit a modest scrap of cover where a rooster had lit earlier in the day. We no more than got up to the edge of the mixed hardwoods when a bird flushed dead away. Don yanked the trigger, then furiously pumped his gun. He repeated this process twice more but no bird! We marked the feathered rocket's end flight as best we could and decided we'd give chase. It would be the last attempt of the day as the burgeoning sun's low, fleeting arc across the sky was coming to an end. Mica was showing the wear and tear of a long afternoon and quite frankly, we were pretty tuckered out too. The dog hesitantly worked along and finally got birdy around a big hump of earth at the edge of an alfalfa field. Don went one way, Justin the other and I stayed behind covering the back door. Wouldn't you know it, that bird held tighter than a tick on a dog's back and finally busted out of the cover headed right back at me. I let it pass by me and break out into the open field when instinct took over swinging the muzzle of my 12 gauge through the bird, which crumpled on the shot, cartwheeling to a stop in the legumes.

We probably should've and could've taken another pheasant or two, but that is not what the day was all about. We had a great time, the three of us enjoying each other's company, the game and the countryside. The dog worked nicely and Justin not only harvested his first pheasant, he took home a pair. I felt a sense of accomplishment knowing that his initial tutelage in the ways of quacking hovercraft, startling flushes and cackling takeoffs was a complete success! The traditions of the outdoor sporting life had been handed off to yet another generation. As we returned to our vehicle for the ride home, the sun was just going down behind the hills of the Finger Lakes, just as it has for thousands of years, and it is one sunset that I will never forget.

CHAPTER 16

Just a Short Walk in the Woods

The calendar indicated it was early March, the 8th to be exact but the thermometer read seventy degrees Fahrenheit. Pretty darn warm for upstate New York in late winter and in fact, it broke a record. I'd had a productive day at the office and come mid-afternoon I decided to take a little leave and head for home. It was so nice outside that I just had to grab my bow, a judo tipped arrow and head for the wilds. I didn't have any destination in mind or any particular thing I wanted to accomplish, so I told the family I'd be back in awhile and took off for a short walk in the woods.

I'm embarrassed to say that I hadn't strung my bow for months, except to shoot a few arrows the prior evening. The previous December, I tore up my ankle playing basketball and was in a cast for four weeks. After ridding myself of that God-forsaken thing, I spent another month and a half in a brace. Add to that the fact that when winter finally came, it came hard. We had several feet of snow on the ground for the better part of January and February.

Finally though, my ankle had healed and the lengthening daylight hours and warm temperatures took their toll on our midwinter blanket.

To say that I was hankering to get out, stretch my legs and do a little stump shooting would be an understatement. So off I went on a very casual walk, a saunter, through the mixed hardwoods covering the kames and kettles behind my house. My mind immediately focused on the abundant deer sign, readily apparent before spring green up. Well-worn trails, that looked as though they should have deer standing in them, traversed the steep hillsides in all the usual places. Strolling along without a care in the world, I flushed a grouse out of its late day dining hall. I'm sure it was searching for any morsel it could find, given the time of year. The smorgasbord of last fall had pretty much disappeared. Swelling buds, a few brave insects and spring's first succulent shoots of vegetation were just starting to supplement last year's beechnuts, samaras and a few, not so well preserved, apples. As luck would have it, that grouse seemed to want to go where I was headed and I flushed the drummer two more times before we parted ways.

I was approaching the transition zone where one of my many treestands is hung, the place where I had taken a plump little eight-pointer the prior fall. Ambling my way through the ash, maple and cherry trees, I picked a leaf here and a twig there and loosed a few arrows. Good shots for the most part considering my lack of muscle tone and practice. I was just a few paces away from my autumnal outpost when I noticed a couple of late season rubs. Late season because they weren't there when I was hunting the area and that the bark, which had been stripped from the tree, still laid atop the previously fallen leaves. A handful of scrapes, both real and not so real, were still evident in the frost heaved, friable soil. At this point, it occurred to me to search for the broadhead end of the arrow that harvested last year's buck. The arrow had passed completely through the deer and snapped off a couple of inches above the broadhead. I had looked for it shortly after recovering my buck but to no avail. After replaying the still vivid incident in my mind, I initiated a search for the cast away Zwickey Eskimo. As I slowly traced the deer's path of egress, from the spot where it last stood, the broadhead materialized, rusted, but otherwise intact. Picking it up, like found treasure, I studied what time and the elements had done to it, and then slipped it into my shirt pocket.

With bounty in hand, sort of speak, I plucked a judo equipped cedar shaft from the quiver and searched for a suitable target. I made a perfect twenty-yard shot down a steep slope, just like one would take from a treestand. After recovering my arrow, I took up my roaming ways, again with no specific heading in mind. Crossing a well-used snowmobile trail, I gazed up a moderate slope and spied a very familiar figure lying on the flattened, decaying leaves covering the forest floor. My heart rate quickened and I literally jogged to my newfound prize, actually looking around to see if anyone was watching. I picked the object up immediately and noticed its heft and the fact that it was in almost perfect condition. It possessed five distinct points, was of moderate length and had a portion of its terminal end broken off. Folks don't find many sheds in this portion of the state. The vast majority of deer in this area are taken at a year and a half of age. Most of those that make it through the general season don't possess a rack of this quality. So this was very special, especially since it was within a hundred steps of my treestand.

As I held the shed antler in my hand, I thought back to last fall and a buck that I had spied about a mile away from my home. It was the peak of the rut and he was tending a doe in the middle of a wide-open hay field just before dark. He was a good buck; one that I thought might make Pope and Young. I never saw him again, but I can still picture him standing there in all his glory, sporting a well-proportioned ten-point rack. Chances are that this was his antler. And being the optimist that I am, I'd like to think that he is alive and well and still in the neighborhood.

With a slight overdose of enthusiasm, I started to look for the other half. What are the odds? My eyes darted from wayward branch, to shadow and back again when I suddenly pushed a deer from some nearby underbrush. It stood there looking over its shoulder at me before bounding away. Could it possibly have been him? If so, will we have another encounter? Will it be next fall? Only time will tell!

I took up my trek once again when my eyes were forced skyward by skeins of geese that coursed overhead buoyed by the abnormally warm vernal thermals. But as they flew toward the horizon, my gaze drifted downward to the ground around me, as I searched the sylvan slopes hoping to find my antler's mate. No luck! I'd just have to come back and take up the hunt another time.

My little jaunt brought me to a long, narrow, old meadow where the timothy, orchard grass and goldenrod had been leveled by the weight of winter's snow. Looking toward the opposite end of the field, I spied a large anthill standing all by itself. It was a perfect target for a quick game of archery golf. I sent an arrow toward the heavens and watched it arc earthward silhouetted against the setting sun. It carried some two hundred yards, nearly forty strides short of its intended mark. Easing the shaft from the ground, I cleaned the newly pulled soil sample from the prongs of the judo. Picking a spot in the middle of the mound, I pulled up and instinctively let go of the bowstring centering the formicary!

I took up my journey back toward the house when a pair of mallards whistle winged overhead headed for some pothole in the middle of a spent cornfield. Arriving at my humble abode I eased up the steps of the porch, hung up my bow and slipped off my boots before retreating inside. I hid my prizes as I entered in order to reveal them at the appropriate moment in my recount of the afternoon's happenings. My family was thrilled with my good fortune and took great joy in "knowing" that a big buck was haunting the woods out back. It's usually these small pleasures in life that are the most memorable and important. I have to continually drum that into my head, due to the fact that they are so easily overlooked. Fortunately, though, sometimes all it takes is just a short walk in the woods to bring you home.

CHAPTER 17

Ruff Guidin'

Fighting his way to a small clearing, the young man pushed through the thick underbrush, which was situated in prime grouse habitat, thicker than an Amazonian jungle and bristling with things that impaled his arms, hands and legs. He stopped for a moment knowing that a bird might take flight at any second. Contemplating his next move he hoped to pick a better way out then he had on the way in. As he took a step toward his intended route, a ruffed grouse hurdled skyward. The cover was so tight that the bird went up like a whirligig, in a nearly vertical fashion. While mounting his gun, pointing it roughly in the direction of the aerial target, the bird seemed to start an inverted loop to the right, not unlike a barnstormer looking to impress his audience. The bolt action 20 gauge was touched off hurtling hundreds of lead pellets through the branches, leaves and boughs of nearby trees. However, not one of them touched their intended mark. The young lad immediately slouched, head down, wanting to crawl away in shame. This quest was extremely important to him, for reasons he still doesn't fully comprehend, and he was not doing very well. The unharmed bird was the thirteenth in a row that he had hunted up, had a good shot at and missed. Thirteen! He had taken grouse before and the game was not a new one but he was in a serious slump that had taken up long-term residence between his ears.

I can look back on this now and smile. And I have certainly related it many times to friends and family. Well, at least friends; family members hunting with me at the time don't let me live it down. To be truthful, I cannot recollect the circumstances surrounding the taking of the next bird that mercifully ended the streak. I was a teenager at the time and a long way from where I am today philosophically, emotionally and in shooting ability. I choose to divulge this anecdote at this time to highlight the fact that my grouse hunting had very humble beginnings, but I stuck with it.

Over the succeeding years, I acquired guns more suitable to the task, new dogs and hundreds of hours of field experience; and by the time I reached my mid-twenties, I considered myself proficient in the finding and taking of ruffed grouse. In fact, for several years at the peak of my grouse hunting pursuits, I kept a journal of my jaunts afield and, over those years, I bagged a solid fifty percent of all the birds shot at. Some may have required two or more shells but they ended up in the game pouch nonetheless. When conversing with other bird hunters afflicted by the magic of the drummer, this average has been looked on as pretty darn good! I attribute this success more to my ability to find birds and understand their habits and idiosyncrasies, than to any shooting prowess I may possess. Due to my knack of locating birds, I usually never had any trouble finding someone to accompany me to the woods when the situation presented itself. However, most of my serious years chasing partridge were conducted as a solitary shootist, albeit for the company of an English springer spaniel or German shorthaired pointer. But what good is developing a skill if you can't share it with someone? So, given my capacity to find grouse hotspots, I have taken a myriad of folks out in search of ol' ruff. Now I don't want to give anyone the wrong impression: I have never been a licensed guide, but I have had enough confidence in my facility to produce results that I have never steered clear of an opportunity to take someone to the grouse woods. And those trips afield have produced some special memories for me as well as for those who have joined me.

A few years back I befriended a colleague who wanted to chase partridge. Don had hunted pheasants back home in Ohio but he had never experienced brush bustin' for grouse so I invited him over to my place and told him to bring a gun he could shoulder quickly and his walking boots and we'd see what we could do. We hadn't been in the woods more than twenty minutes when I came to a great grouse haunt. Knowing I could push at least one bird out of it, I set Don up on a trail that led to open hardwoods. As we eased along, sure enough, the dog put one up — it flew away from me, and angled out in front of Don. Clearing the thick stuff, it turned and went right down the trail toward the hardwoods. This presented Don with an atypical opportunity to harvest a grouse, a wide-open shot. Boom, boom — nothing! The bird glided away careening through the trees in search of a safe haven. We hunted on.

After a few more close calls in heavy cover, I thought of another sure-fire spot for Don to get his first grouse. A thick, thorny hillside usually produced a bird and if we worked it right, we could put one out over a grassy meadow for wide-open shooting. After Don got positioned in the field, the dog and I penetrated the labyrinth of brush. She worked beautifully, plowing her way through or under alders, honeysuckle and all manner of prickly protuberances. Just as we approached the bottom of the slope, a bird exploded from the cover at a forty-five degree angle and leveled out over the meadow flying directly at Don. Three shots rang out in rapid succession; the bird never flinched and soared away to the hemlock tops across a creek. This probably doesn't seem all that extraordinary but in each instance, I had accurately predicted that a bird would emerge, what it would do and where it would go. Prognostication like this comes by way a sixth sense developed from knowing the birds, their habitat and having blown chances at taking grouse out of these coverts in the past!

Taking a friend to the grouse woods is one thing and taking your son is quite another. Justin had just cut his teeth on bird hunting by experiencing some invigorating waterfowling over decoys. So I told him that in order to get a grouse we had to switch from the "they come to you mode" to the "we go to them mode." Having ducks hovering in the air over decoy-laced water though is very different from having a grouse launch itself, unseen, from thick underbrush, not unlike a winged cannonball. Justin's first opportunity at a bird came shortly into his inaugural hunt. He had crashed down a steep hill that I was sure would produce a flush and hit the bottom when a partridge took off, practically from beneath his feet. I yelled "BIRD" and his gun started up, but he never sorted his objective out of the brushy tangle thereby holding his fire. Bird one, guide and son, zero.

We continued on, picking our way through some mediocre cover when we came to another one of my honey holes. A brushy field edge provided a perfect set up for Justin to take his first *Bonasa umbellus*. I put the young hunter out in the field and told him to mirror my progress through the cover. "Don't fall behind, and don't get out ahead," I instructed. Again, the plan worked perfectly, although the bird never broke out of the brush to offer Justin a shot. But I was on my game and tracked the bird's flight to a hemlock grove a few hundred feet ahead.

We regrouped just before entering the dark, dank cathedral of trees. As a guide, I felt it necessary to point out a few scenarios that might take place. One, the bird would probably fly out well ahead of us, because it had been rousted from its security blanket. Second, it could have flown into one of the towering trees and would either never move, or take off with a lot of air between him and the gun.

Last, it could hold tight, let us pass by, and then slip away behind us. After enumerating each of these possibilities, Justin and I quietly entered the bird's sanctuary. We hadn't gone far when the bird revealed its plan. The pat chose option three, attempting to duck out the back door. It was a long shot, one that could be made, but long and because Justin was still learning the game, the bird escaped unscathed, although the gun had been fired in its general direction. Guiding is all about finding birds, not bagging them — right?

Fortunately, not all my guiding results in a lack of feathers in the game pouch. I have taken numerous family members and friends out and gotten a number of birds. Probably the most memorable though, to this point, was a trip to the woods a few years ago with my young nephew Steven. He was a relatively new hunter at the time and had been out chasing ducks, grouse and other feathered fowl but had yet to collect a partridge. I took Steve to a familiar patch of real estate that had consistently produced birds in the past. On all of my previous hunts, I had approached the covert from the west and each time, birds would get up and loop backward toward denser cover. Patches of tall hemlock grew in this particular locale and the birds were quite adept at putting one or more of them between the hunter and themselves, therefore I rarely took a bird out of there. Given this past experience, Steve and I stalked the area from the east. It was a gloomy, overcast day, which improved our chances greatly. We were hunting in the waning hours of the afternoon and had the skies been clear, the sun would have been directly in our eyes. As we hit the edge that had so often produced birds, I advised Steve to line himself up so that he had a lane or two to shoot down. I told him we'd probably put one out sooner rather than later and it would fly straight away through the hemlocks. My springer spaniel proved me right and flushed a grouse as if on cue. The bird flew right in front of Steve and leveled off quickly. He was up for the task though, squeezed the trigger and downed it with one shot, his first pat! I'm not sure that Steve ever thought of me as a grouse guide. In fact, I'm confident that he did not. However, he has always remembered getting his first drummer with me and the fact that I called it as if I had planned it, just as a grouse guide would!

CHAPTER 18

An Almost Perfect Morning

Justin and I had successfully stalked our treestands, which hung together from a clump of trees in an area where the deer activity had been steady since the beginning of the bow season. He snuck in the back door while I went around through a side door laying down a doe-in-heat scent trail and spicing up a licking branch over a well-used scrape. We rendezvoused at our clump of trees and carefully climbed into our stands set side by side at a height of fifteen feet. Justin had turned twelve the previous summer and this was his third autumn accompanying me in my pursuit of whitetails. We had experienced a lot together in the past, always having a good time, thus keeping his enthusiasm high enough to get up in the wee hours of the morning to go hunting with me. I stood, bow in hand, and Justin sat in the darkness waiting for the dawning of another early November day. The southwest wind was perfect for the spot we were in and the temperature was comfortable enough for an extended wait. We hadn't been there ten minutes though when we heard a deer break over the ridge to the west and head in our general direction. By the steady grunting emanating from its position, it was no doubt a buck. Even though it was yet to get light enough for good shooting, I grunted back at him and made a few estrous doe bleats. The only response I got was a few grunts and a rustling noise from the dry leaves blanketing the forest floor in his vicinity. This went on for several minutes and then everything went quiet on the hillside above us.

As the first hint of light began to illuminate the east-facing slope, we studied it intently for anything that looked like a deer or any part thereof. Nothing! It was at this point that a chorus of calls from several turkeys began to serenade us from the same ridge where we had heard the buck. As the turkey calls reached a crescendo in the growing daylight, the birds began to fly down onto the spine of the ridge. Justin was enthralled at the sight of this spectacle. He had seen and heard turkeys before but now he had a front row seat to something most people never experience. Bird after bird flew down, and as they did, an adult hen began to yelp. To say that she was insistent is an understatement. I have heard scores of turkeys making every conceivable sound they make but this hen was yelping louder, longer and more constant than any I have ever heard. It was as though someone had put a "how to sound like a hen turkey yelp" album (CD to the youngsters) on a stereo, cranked the volume up and left it on the ridge top. While all this was going on, we heard turkeys behind us and out in front of us down in what I call the bottom, a small valley cloaked by old apple trees and honeysuckle brush. We were surrounded!

Shortly thereafter, a sound caught my attention, coming from my right and slightly behind me. I eased my head around to see a plump, mature, solitary doe standing motionless a mere fifteen yards away. Man, can they be quiet when they want to be. She looked down and began to walk along a well-used deer trail. She crossed Justin's entry trail into the stand but never picked up his scent. Somebody taught him that it is always wise to wear rubber bottom boots and not touch anything when entering a stand location. The doe continued to walk parallel to our position until she cut my trail laced with doe-in-heat scent. At that point, she acted more like a bird dog on a fresh grouse trail than a deer and made a ninety-degree turn toward our position. Ending up on the scrape, where I had been just a short time earlier, she sucked in the aroma of the lure that I had left on the overhanging branch. She offered several excellent shot opportunities, but this was not my intended quarry on this outing. The doe hung around for several minutes before easing off toward the bottom where we lost track of her in the thick brush.

As morning eased along, Justin noticed movement, this time it was behind us and to our left. Looking out of the corner of his eye, he saw several figures picking their way along in our direction and whispered "Dad, turkeys!" I slowly turned my eyes toward the birds, spying several toms coming toward our little hideaway. Since the season was open and I had a tag in my possession, I was going through some mental gymnastics to decide whether to shoot one or not. But as has consistently been my experience, when sitting in a treestand, those birds picked us out like an ermine in the middle of a pool table. I knew the jig was up when I heard three or four quick clucks as the birds veered away from us and headed into a thicket.

Within minutes of our close encounter with Ben Franklin's favorite birds, a motion down in the bottom confirmed that several does and fawns were moving up slope toward the ridge. They climbed steadily higher, and then turned south away from us. Shortly after they passed, what I thought was a straggler following them up the hill turned out to be a small buck. He ambled up the same trail but stopped a few times to leave scent posts and paw in the leaves making several halfhearted scrapes. When he got to the point where the does and fawns had gone southward, he turned and proceeded in a northerly direction. He'd gone about thirty yards when another deer suddenly charged out from behind a large deadfall and gave chase to the small buck, which retreated in the direction of the does and fawns. They both went out of sight but we could hear them making tracks in the crisp autumn leaves as they went. In a few minutes, the mystery deer returned. I knew it had to be a bigger buck but really didn't get a good look at him as he ran the smaller buck off. When he returned, I saw that it was a big ten-point that I had seen earlier in the season. It was a good buck, a very good buck! He retreated to the area near the deadfall when I surmised that this was the buck that Justin and I had heard just after we had gotten into our stands. He must have come over the ridge and bedded down on the hillside, tucking himself away behind the deadfall. Evidently, he had been there the entire morning.

The ten-point wasn't in a hurry to do anything in particular. He obviously did not want the small buck around, but he also didn't feel like chasing does; they had passed right by him earlier with no reaction on his part. He started to browse, taking a few steps in our direction as he did. Things had quieted down some so I decided to see if I could pique the buck's attention and move him in our direction. I had a good trail laid out between him and us that might gain his interest if he came our way, so I serenaded him with a few doe bleats and tending grunts. The big boy didn't appear to hear them or if he did, he didn't act as though he cared. I went though my imitations again, and again he paid absolutely no attention. He continued to browse and look around moving ever so slowly down the slope toward us.

While this was playing out, I whispered words of encouragement to the buck to come down and join us, as well as telling Justin that this could come together at any second. I'm not sure if I was trying to convince him or me, but it was fun doing play by play into my son's ear as things unfolded. Throughout the morning we had been quietly chatting about all that we were experiencing and it was obvious to me that Justin was fully engaged as the minutes melted into hours. I started to reflect on how much he had learned about the woods and its inhabitants and how in tune he was with all of it. He was even starting to spot game before I would — which bodes well for his future as a bowhunter. Just two more years and he'll have a bow in his hand, but until then, his tutelage continues.

I kept "persuading" the ten-point down the hill but he had not made much progress toward that end. Justin then informed me that a flock of turkeys was moving up out of the bottom toward us. There was a bunch of them, steadily walking up an ascending ridge parallel to our position. Since I keep a bowhunter's log of game observed while in the field for our state fish and game department, I told Justin to pick out a landmark and count the birds as they passed by it. I turned to locate the buck to see that he was still milling around near the deadfall. Justin had counted the fourth bird when all of a sudden a very familiar sound caught our attention. An animal was steadily walking toward us from our rear flank. Whether it's experience, intuition or what exactly, I don't know, but I just knew that the animal was a whitetail buck. He would have to come directly upwind to us in order for me to get a crack at him. Since our stands are located on the edge of a small bowl deer often come in from that direction without winding us due to the fortuitous lay of the land. I turned to confirm what I had expected: a nice eight-point was fast approaching. Remarkably, I was familiar with this deer as well. He had come into this same stand earlier in the season and walked right through a shooting lane at the edge of my effective range. After passing on that somewhat iffy opportunity, I later wondered if I could have managed a good shot. But that was history and now it looked as though he was going to give me a second chance, albeit from the opposite direction.

I'd like to think that he had heard my simulations, consisting of doe bleats and tending buck grunts, and come in to investigate. But that didn't really matter as he passed by a large cluster of trees some sixteen yards away while at the same time I prepared for the impending shot. Clearing the trees, he kept up his steady pace, scanning the woods in front of him. I started to pull back and almost got to full draw as he topped the small knoll we were on, but he kept on walking. Letting the bow down, I made a fawn bleat with my mouth to stop him. He continued on his way. As he got to the scrape I had doctored up hours earlier, he finally came to a halt. At this point, I was on automatic pilot after having nearly been to full draw then at half draw for what seemed like minutes, but what was in reality, only a few seconds. When the tip of the middle finger of my string hand tickled the whiskers of my mustache, the Zwickey tipped arrow leapt from my bow toward the buck. I wanted this moment to come together more than any other I can think of. Justin and I had experienced a perfect morning. The game we saw around us the entire time that we were there, opportunities passed up for a better one, and just plain enjoying this time together could all be topped off with the successful harvest of this buck. A buck that wasn't huge by any means but was a nice, mature whitetail sporting a typical eight-point rack.

The release of the arrow felt good, and its flight was perfect, perfectly over the buck's back by about an inch and a half. I think I said it aloud, "Oh no!" The buck took two bounds, stopped and looked back at us. The turkeys scurried some, but didn't spook. Everything froze, except for my pounding heart and racing mind, which was trying to figure out how I could miss an ideal, sixteen-yard shot at a broadside standing buck that had absolutely no clue we were there. After what seemed like an eternity, the buck turned and slowly walked down toward the bottom. The turkeys resumed their trek up the hill and I looked to see the big ten-point watch, then join the eight-point and disappear into the brush some one hundred yards below us. I slumped down into the seat of my treestand, leaned over to my son, and told him that I was sorry. "Sorry, for what? That was great!" Justin said. He didn't feel badly, except for feeling badly for me. He knew how much I wanted to be successful with him as a witness. We had been close before. I'd taken bucks the previous two years that he's been going out with me but not while he was in the tree with me. School and a head cold had thwarted our efforts in the past.

After our little incident, the woods seemingly became devoid of life, but we hung in there. Or should I say, I hung in there for a while, and then got down to retrieve my arrow. Unfortunately this was not the first time I plucked an arrow from the moist forest floor and tried to figure out how it got from where I was to where it was without going through the deer that had been standing there: Unbelievable! Justin and I gathered up our gear and headed for home, with me verbally kicking myself in the butt all the way there.

To say I was a little disappointed in myself and frustrated with what had happened might be an understatement and my attitude probably needed some readjusting. The next morning the wind gods were kind enough to allow me to hunt the same stand, even though I knew deep down inside that might not be a good decision. After a quick shower, I checked with Justin to see if he was game. He'd had a very busy week and thought he might better sleep in, and he did. I never pressure him to go, I might make my case, but I never lay any guilt trips on him. So, off I went to relive the previous day's adventures and miscue on my own. Not surprisingly, things were slow — somehow; I knew they would be. I only saw a few does and fawns and again passed on a mature doe, which I hoped might act as bait for one of the area's bucks, as she hung around for quite a while. As the remainder of that Sunday wore on, I continued to talk to myself about what had happened, sometimes under my breath, sometimes not. My family is used to these events and even tries to console me at times. At other times, they just clue me in, as only they can do, on just what really is important in life.

It was about halftime of whatever NFL game was on that day when I decided that I certainly wouldn't be filling my tag from the living room. Given the northwest wind that was blowing, I was limited to which afternoon stand I could hunt. Earlier in the season, on a whim, I set a stand directly behind my house, literally within a stone's throw of my backdoor. That stand can only be hunted on a northwest wind in the afternoon. With that in mind, I got my gear together and was in the stand within minutes.

I really didn't think that I would get an opportunity from that stand. Having hunted it a couple of times before, I had only seen a few does and fawns. In order to increase my odds, I laid out a scent trail and hung the drag pad on a small branch. I hadn't been in the stand thirty minutes when on the hill to the east a small buck appeared. Given the fact that I don't travel extensively to hunt whitetails and try my best to harvest one "in my own woodlot," I know from experience that you don't always have the luxury to be picky, so I'm not. After the buck flirted with my scent stream on several occasions and started moving in my general direction, I prepared myself for a potential shot opportunity. I'm not sure if he had gotten a whiff of my scent post or just didn't want to enter the adjacent meadow in the waning light of day. But whatever the reason, he hung around for several minutes, seemingly not in any hurry to go anywhere in particular. Eventually he went under an old pasture fence, right where he was supposed to, and came my way. He eased his way closer and closer, never offering a shot until he stopped six yards away, right below my perch in the woods. Maybe it's just me but I couldn't pass up a six-yard broadside shot at a buck totally oblivious of my presence. My Great Northern Super Ghost came to full draw and the two-bladed broadhead tipped cedar shaft was on its way before I knew it.

The shot was flawless and the buck crashed off, arcing uphill away from me. I was so confident in the hit that I immediately got down and went to get Justin. After he got his stuff on and grabbed an extra flashlight, we went to trail the buck. Justin was thrilled with my good fortune as we cautiously followed the spoor. Even though I surmised that the buck had expired before I got out of the stand, I didn't want to press my luck. I would work the trail out and Justin would benchmark the last sign. I'd go a ways then he would join me. The buck went up a hill, through a saddle and down the other side. We had gone more than two hundred yards from where the buck was when I shot him and I was starting to wonder if the shot was as good as I thought. With light quickly fading, I looked down toward the bottom of the hill and caught a glimpse of white hair in the honeysuckle brush. Justin had not yet seen the deer, so I had him join me and asked him to take up the trail. He went another twenty steps or so when I saw him snap to attention as he spotted the buck laying a short distance in front of him. Looking back at me, he exclaimed, "Dad, there he is!"

I was glad to have gotten the deer. My entire family enjoys venison and this would be a nice addition to our table fare. Justin helped me with the field dressing chores and dragging him out. It was at this point that I told him that all he had to do was put our experiences the day before and that evening together and he got the entire picture. He then looked up at me and said, "Yeah dad, but I didn't actually see you shoot the deer!" What do you say to a twelve year old except, "Oh well, maybe next year?"

Epilogue

"In the woods, we return to reason and faith."
— Ralph Waldo Emerson

Stepping outside, I immediately take note of the substantive chill in the air. Striding purposely across my wooded yard, I stop to feel the northwest wind buffet my bearded face and look skyward to admire the azure blue sky speckled with pure white, popcorn-like cumulus clouds that drift slowly to the south and east. My gaze is diverted to the red, yellow and orange leaves of the maple, birch and hickory trees that surround me, their arms radiating toward the heavens. Perfectly shaped water droplets dangle from their leaf tips, sparkling in the early morning sunlight like diamonds hanging from a pretty girl's ears. There's a familiar tickle in my nostrils as I breathe in the musky aroma of decomposing vegetation and the dank smell of the soil as it struggles to warm up from last night's frost. Suddenly my interest is piqued as the faint sound of honking Canada geese creeps into my consciousness growing louder as they cruise along just above the treetops. Noticing something unexpected on the ground, I bend down to pick it up and smooth it between my fingers. A ruffed grouse has passed this way, as its lone tail feather suggests. I test the sharpness of its quill and then stroke the soft, delicate vanes of its squared end. It looks like a hen's feather given the fuzziness of the band that extends its breadth. Releasing the feather, I watch as it falls back to Mother Earth when my stomach grumbles as if it requires nourishment. It seems as though I'm always hungry this time of year. It must have something to do with links to my prehistoric ancestors and their need to fatten up for a long winter ahead. The sights, the sounds, the smells all point to the same end — autumn has arrived and with it, a time to harvest what God has placed before me. It is a time to reap, not only in a physical sense, but also spiritually, a time to be thankful for the out-of-doors — the trees, the hills, and the wild creatures that roam throughout — and a time to appreciate life itself and the beauty of Nature. So go, find the wilds, find yourself and enjoy!

So go,

find the wilds,

find yourself

and enjoy!

About the Author

Bruce A. Hopkins, a lifelong outdoor enthusiast and freelance writer, has contributed articles to a number of periodicals including *Traditional Bowhunter, The Professional Bowhunter Magazine* and *Full Draw*. A practicing conservationist, Hopkins is employed by the Natural Resources Conservation Service and is responsible for administering numerous programs that protect, restore and enhance wetlands, stream corridors and wildlife habitat. Selected as a Congressional Fellow, Hopkins served as a staff member to the U.S. Senate Committee on Agriculture, Nutrition and Forestry where he worked on a variety of natural resource conservation issues. He is a member of numerous sporting and conservation organizations including the Professional Bowhunters Society, Pope and Young Club, Rocky Mountain Elk Foundation, Ruffed Grouse Society, Ducks Unlimited, Pheasants Forever and New York Bowhunters. Hopkins resides and recreates in rural central New York with his wife, Beth; daughter, Melissa; son, Justin and mother, Marjorie.

GIVE THE GIFT OF
SHOTSHELLS AND CEDAR SHAFTS
TO YOUR FAMILY, FRIENDS, AND COLLEAGUES

■ **Email Orders:** hoppy5979@msn.com

■ **Telephone Orders:** Call (315) 821-7120.
Have your credit card ready.

■ **Postal Orders:** Cassety Hollow Publishing
P.O. Box 415
Oriskany Falls, NY 13425-0415

■ **Please send ____ book(s) to:**

Name:_____

Address: _____

City: _____State: ____Zip:_____

Telephone: (   )_____

Email:_____

■ **Price: $23.95** Contact publisher for quantity orders.

■ **Shipping:** $4.00; Each additional copy: $2.00

New York residents must add sales tax on books and shipping.

■ **Payment:**

❑ Check #_____   ❑ Money Order # _____

❑ Mastercard ❑ Visa
Card Number: _____Exp. Date _____

Cardholder Signature: _____

Make check or money order payable to:
Cassety Hollow Publishing

Book(s) will be personalized
Indicate name of person(s) to be addressed to:

_____